THE
EASTER
MYSTERIES

BEATRICE
BRUTEAU

A Crossroad Book
The Crossroad Publishing Company
New York

1995

The Crossroad Publishing Company
370 Lexington Avenue, New York, NY 10017

Copyright © 1995 by Beatrice Bruteau

Printed in the United States of America

Library of Congress Cataloging-in-Publication Data

Bruteau, Beatrice, 1930–
    The Easter mysteries / Beatrice Bruteau.
        p.   cm.
    ISBN 0-8245-1493-9 (pbk.)
        1. Lent—Prayer-books and devotions—English.   2. Paschal mystery—Prayer-books and devotions—English.   3. Catholic Church—Prayer-books and devotions—English.   I. Title.
BX2170.14B78   1995
242'.34–dc20

95-4710
                                                                            CIP

CONTENTS

━━━━━━━━━ ஒ ━━━━━━━━━

PREFACE

━━━━━━━━━━━━━━ ⍦ ━━━━━━━━━━━━━━

I N THESE REFLECTIONS I have been concerned mainly to stress
that the mysteries are intended to bring us into a lived experience of the sacred reality of which they are revelations. I
am afraid that many people don't understand how the mysteries
are supposed to work. The most profound and awesome rites,
for which our ancestors prepared with all-absorbing prayer and
fasting, are now routine rituals that we walk through with very
little consciousness. So much of our religion is either legalism,
social habit, family tradition, or ethnic identity. All of these
are travesties of the original intention of the mysteries to be an
utterly transforming contact with the Transcendent.

In a culture in which practically no hint of the sacred remains, I believe we must make a grand effort to reclaim or
re-create a mystery entrance to the *metanoia,* the transformed
consciousness that alone makes our lives meaningful and satisfying by putting us in touch with the deepest truths of existence.

There must be a great many ways to do this. I am using traditional Christian materials familiar to, and precious to, many
people in this culture. I share what these mysteries mean to me.
But I hope that the ideas raised, and especially the exercises proposed, will be starting points for readers to discover their own
meanings by having their own experiences.

My thought is that you might use this book during the weeks
before and after Easter, reading it chapter by chapter and practicing the exercises every day. I do believe that if you read merely
to see what the author has to say, without doing the exercises

7

(or something rather like them) sincerely for yourselves, it will not be at all the same experience. After all, the whole point is to attain one's own experience of God.

In this context, I would also say that the lapsed time is part of the program. Don't read ahead; you need to live with the thoughts and the practices and let time pass in your body and your unconscious mind. Practice every day. Continue practicing after finishing the book. Do the whole thing over again next year, using your own improvements on the course.

Finally, I would hope that this approach would encourage the reader to search out the mystery treasures in other traditional materials — texts, doctrines, legends, icons, music, liturgy, devotions. Remember that their surface meaning is not their whole story. Historical, devotional, moral meanings do not exhaust them. They may have several layers of revelation artfully concealed until our spiritual discernment can uncover them. It is my belief that all the revelations apply to ourselves. I often say of a Bible story that it is not just about a couple of other people a long time ago. It is about you; all the characters can be found in you, in your interior life. If you will work with our heritage in this way, I believe you will find endless beautiful things.

When you do see something, receive a "light," have some breakthrough, "come alive" in a new way, be sure that you protect this gift, nourish it, put it into practice. This is what I like to call "feeding the daughter of Jairus" (Mark 5:43). If you are faithful in this way with even small gifts that you are given, you will be preparing yourself for greater gifts.

If we open ourselves to the revelations in this way, we may be able to know again the awesome power that is there in the Easter mysteries.

— One —

THE SACRED MYSTERIES

 ⌘

C HRISTIANITY is a mystery religion. "Mystery" is from the Greek *mystērion*, whose Latin equivalent is *sacramentum*, or sacrament. So when we say that Christianity is a "mystery religion," we mean that it is a sacramental religion. A sacrament is defined in most Christian catechisms as an external and visible sign of an interior and invisible grace. "Grace" means a participation in the life of God, given to us by God as a free gift, not something that comes to us because of our human nature or our behavior. So a mystery religion is one that uses external and visible signs of interior and invisible graces, participations in the divine life.

This is what we are going to be talking about and opening ourselves to experience through the meditations and exercises presented in this book: the interior and invisible graces that are indicated by the sacraments, or mysteries, that are celebrated in the Christian revelation, particularly those connected with Easter.

The most usual sacraments, recognized by almost all Christian communities, are Baptism and Eucharist (or Holy Communion, or the Lord's Supper). Some churches also admit Confirmation, Matrimony, Unction (the anointing of the sick for healing), Penance or Reconciliation (a recognition of God's forgiveness), and Ordination. There was a time in the early days of the Christian church when various other rites were celebrated as sacraments. One of these, which will concern us, is Footwashing.

We are also going to go through the meditational ceremony known as the Stations of the Cross. This is not a sacrament, but the Stations illustrate a secondary meaning of the word "mystery," namely, "sacred event." The outstanding events in the life of Christ are called "mysteries" in this sense. They can also be interpreted as external signs of internal graces, both for him and for us.

Examples of these mysteries are the Annunciation, when Jesus was conceived by the Blessed Virgin Mary; the Visitation, when John the Baptist and his mother, Elizabeth, recognized the presence of the Lord even before his birth; the Nativity, or birth of Jesus in Bethlehem, which we now celebrate as Christmas; the Baptism of Jesus by John in the River Jordan, followed by his fast in the wilderness and his rejection of the Temptations; the Marriage Feast at Cana and the first of the identifying "works"; the Transfiguration, when Jesus was perceived in intense light conversing with Moses (who represents the Law) and Elijah (who represents the Prophets).

There are many other examples. Each of these sacred events is a revelation of an important truth about our relation to God. If we meditate on them and absorb the truth they enshrine, we will participate more fully in the divine life. The mysteries turn the jewel of the revelation, so to speak, and show the various facets of it, but the revelation is itself a single great truth.

All the mysteries are related to the fundamental sacred event, which is the transforming death/resurrection mystery. It is this mystery into which we are called to enter, to undergo the transformation that it promises. Undergoing the transformation means leaving our old life and beginning a new life. We are initiated into newness of life. "Initiation" is the root meaning of *mystērion*. It means to learn a secret, something told with "closed lips." This suggests to me a revelation of what is essentially unspeakable, something for which there are no words, something that cannot be transmitted through the medium of language.

I believe that this is so, that the Ultimate Mystery cannot be told. Nevertheless, we are going to talk about it, and I will propose certain practices and meditations that may help to relax some of the barriers that we all seem to have between us and the realization of the new life. It is these barriers that we have to break down. We presently believe them to be our life, and if we insist on clinging to them — if we attempt to "save our life" — then we will not be able to enter into the new life. But if we lose this old life by embracing the Gospel, then we will find ourselves endowed with eternal life, a life not subject to corruption and decay.

Transformation

Transformation is something we all crave. This is what we are looking for under the guises of the many things we do. We seek fulfillment through security, pleasure, power, personal relationships, artistic creativity, intellectual insight, and mystical experiences. We are intimately familiar with ourselves as beings available for mutation. And yet we also put obstacles in the way of the very transformation we most deeply desire. We really want to lose ourselves, and yet we cling to ourselves. We continue to try to define ourselves, piling up adjectives by which we — and, we hope, *we alone* — can be described; but at the same time we know, on some secret level, that we are indefinable.

But to realize ourselves as indefinable, of course, we would have to stop identifying ourselves by all these descriptions to which we are so attached. You can test this in your own consciousness. Take pen and paper. Ask yourself, "Who am I?" See what springs to mind. Write it down. Ask again and again. Most people automatically begin to describe themselves in terms of their family relationships and their work relationships. Many people will describe themselves in terms of the position or success they have achieved; others by what they perceive as their handicaps. Some of us — more refined souls! — will describe ourselves in terms of our ideals and our aspirations. Now, can we transcend these descriptions? Can we strip ourselves naked of adjectives?

If we do, what will we have left? Nothing, it seems. And that *nothing* is just the point. That is the mystical death that is the flip side of our resurrection and eternal life. It is a drastic and terrifying prospect. At least, it is as long as we cling to these descriptive possessions of ours. This is what is meant by the difficulty of a "rich" person entering the kingdom of heaven (Matt. 19:23–26). Aren't we usually engaged in putting up new and bigger barns to house our accumulated treasures (Luke 12:18–19)? But Jesus plainly warns those who can hear him: "Do not lay up treasures for yourselves on earth" (Matt. 6:19–21). Don't rest your heart in them.

We may have thought that these earthly treasures from which we have been warned off were only money and real estate and fine clothes and art objects and jewelry. But they include, more importantly, whatever we are especially proud of — or, for that matter, ashamed of, or whatever we think sets us apart and *identifies* us. Our earthly treasure is our self-image and our self-esteem. Hard words. Absolutely. Practicing Christianity is like being crucified. Didn't anybody ever tell you?

What are some examples of earthly treasures? All sorts of class memberships, for starters. Ethnic identity, economic class identity, educational level, physical attractiveness, sexual orientation, gender, marital status, age group, political orientation, nationality, church membership. "Do not presume to say to yourselves, 'We have Abraham as our father'; for I tell you, God is able from these stones to raise up children to Abraham" (words of John the Baptist in Matt. 3:8). Belonging to an "in group" will not entitle any of us to self-transcendence and transfiguration. Quite the contrary. Reliance on membership in any group that is separated off from the rest of reality is precisely what prevents us from dying and rising to newness of life.

The revelation from Christ sets our most intimate kin at odds with us: our foes will be members of our own household — that is, our own sense of ourselves, of who we are and why we are important and deserving of respect. These are some of the things that keep us from eternal life. Remember that shame and self-hatred and a strong sense of identity with any separating characteristic are just as much barriers as pride and self-inflation and identification with a power group. This isn't often recognized or stressed, and it is important.

In our unredeemed, or imprisoned, condition, we are trapped in a vicious circle: we keep trying to secure ourselves by piling up things to say about ourselves, to reassure ourselves that we exist, and the more we do this, the more isolated we feel and the more insecure. We try harder and harder to save our lives, and the more we do, the more they seem to slip away from us. We are not really "living," we feel; we are just barely keeping our heads above water. How can we get out of this trap, this prison?

God's Love

The revelation of divine love in Christianity is redemption from this prison. Jesus preaches from beginning to end that God loves each one of us, and *therefore* we have nothing to fear, nothing to protect, nothing to defend, nothing to crave. "I tell you, do not be anxious about your life, what you shall eat or what you shall drink, nor about your body, what you shall put on. Is not life more than food, and the body more than clothing?" (Matt. 6:25).

We keep trying to fatten ourselves with various social, psychological, emotional, intellectual, or esthetic nourishments, making ourselves anxious. We keep trying to clothe ourselves in successes and accomplishments, in masks of various kinds to impress one another — and even ourselves. But life is more im-

portant than these nourishments and the body more valuable
than these costumes. Life and body in this passage mean our
reality, which comes to us directly from God and is the living
proof, from moment to moment, of God's love for us.

The sense of security and satisfaction that we are trying to
achieve by all these efforts is already available to us by realization of God's love for us. What greater security could there be?
What greater success? What greater satisfaction? If we can really
hear this revelation — if we have the "ears" to hear it — then we
can be "saved," "rescued," "redeemed," released from the trap.
It is a kind of awakening, or like suddenly having your eyes
opened though you were born blind. The prison doors mirac-
ulously open — as in the story about St. Peter (Acts 12) — the
shackles fall off, and we are led out into life.

The shackles, the chains, that fall off are our needs to have
this, do that, be something, defend ourselves, protect ourselves,
and so on. All those things that we were so concerned about
suddenly disappear. We see that it is quite unnecessary to bother
ourselves about them at all. That type of self-concern and even
that type of self-awareness vanish. *That life dies at the same
moment that the new life begins.* They are two sides of the
same coin.

The redeeming power of God's love is always there. We have
to be willing to believe it, accept it. Accepting it means that we
no longer try to sustain ourselves, try to make ourselves exist.
That's the giving up of clinging to our life. On the other hand,
once we believe that God loves us, we see right away that all
that clinging was unnecessary anyway, and so it just falls away.

But really being able to believe may not be easy. While we
struggle with it, it is like working ourselves up and down on the
cross: up to breathe, down to rest, pain and stress any way you
move. We may claim that we believe in God's love, but we hedge
our bets just the same by continuing to lay up a little treasure of
the earthly type to make ourselves "feel good about ourselves."
But release into eternal life is not a halfway affair. It is very little
comfort to be only a little imprisoned; to be caught at all is not

to be free. This is why the Christian demand is so exorbitant. *Everything* has to be given up, left behind.

Baptism

How is this revelation of grace made visible by the sacramental celebrations of the Christian community? The death/resurrection transformation that we have been speaking of is figured in the sacrament of Baptism.

> Do you not know that all of us who have been baptized into Christ Jesus were baptized into his death? We were buried...with him by Baptism into death, so that as Christ was raised from the dead by the glory of the Father, we too might walk in newness of life....Our old self was crucified with him so that...we might no longer be enslaved....But if we...have been united with him in a death like his, we shall certainly be united with him in a resurrection like his. (Rom. 6:3–8, with omissions and rearrangement)

The rite of Baptism, especially when practiced by immersion, is a vivid representation of burial and resurrection. Those who witness it see someone disappear under the water (as under the earth) and then come back. But the meaning of the ritual is that the person comes back *changed,* with a different life principle. For the persons being baptized, the experience may be even more vivid, depending on how long they are held under the water!

The story is told of a spiritual teacher who was asked by a disciple how great should be his desire for God. The teacher took the disciple down to the river, and they waded out to the deep, where the teacher suddenly seized the disciple and held him under the water until he struggled violently to raise his head. When the disciple had recovered himself a bit, the teacher asked, "While you were under the water, what did you want most?" "A breath of air!" the disciple replied. "When you want

God's grace that much," said the teacher, "you will have no difficulty receiving it."

"Ask, and you shall receive," said Jesus (Matt. 7:7). But really *ask!* Ask as if for the only thing you want. This is what we may deeply experience when we are baptized. Cleansed and renewed, we feel reborn, emerging from a divine womb with a new kind of life. If we have already been ritually baptized, we can still have this experience by meditating on the Easter mystery, by entering into it interiorly, renewing and deepening our baptismal transformation.

Notice how the mystery works: the sacrament both *represents,* in a graphic and dramatic way, the grace it conveys and also *creates* an event-situation or experience that predisposes the person receiving the sacrament to realize the grace. Baptism represents burial and resurrection, and the shock and fear of being under the water has some emotional resonance with self-loss, followed by the renewal of drawing breath again. We say the sacrament actually effects what it represents. The representation is the external and visible sign. The effect is the interior and invisible grace.

The grace is invisible and interior. What does this mean? Let us consult the Gospel according to John, chapter 3, the story of Nicodemus's conversation with Jesus about Baptism. Nicodemus came to Jesus by night — that is, in darkness or ignorance, but he *came,* which indicated that he knew he was ignorant, and this shows in the first thing he says: "Rabbi, we know you have come from God as a *teacher.*" How does he know? "No one would have the power to do the signs that you do unless God was with him." The "signs": he means the miracles, the amazing "works," as Jesus himself called them when he explained that it was the Father, God, dwelling in him who performed these deeds (John 14:10).

This shows that Nicodemus was sensitive to the *mystery* aspect, the sacramental quality, of what Jesus was doing. He knew that these deeds were not merely welcome healings for the people concerned, but had deeper meanings. They carried interior graces, not only for those healed but also for those who witnessed them, or even heard of them at second hand. This sensitivity to the deeper layers, the dimensions at first unnoticed, is what has prepared Nicodemus for his encounter with the divine Teacher.

The Sacred Story

This is a sensitivity that is not common in our culture. It was very common in the ancient world, and that is why those people wrote their literature the way they did. They understood that a sacred story is supposed to mean different things on different levels. You can't just take the surface level; you will miss too much. Sacred Scripture is rather like a hologram. At first sight it is only a smooth, gray level surface, obviously flat. But if you tilt it and let the light shine on it at various angles, you see layer upon layer in three dimensions, level after level of images in it.

This is the sort of thing we have to be on the watch for when we read the ancient literature and when we consider the events of sacred history and their re-presentations in the ritual ceremonies of the church. If we take these things merely "literally," we will miss most of what they have to say to us. If the presentation is highly metaphorical or symbolic, we may miss its point altogether.

It is the misfortune of our culture that we think that something is either physically and literally true or not true at all. The ancient world had a different mentality; their teachers would often communicate a profound meaning by telling a story. The story was what we would call fiction, but what it communicated was very true. Our people tend to read the Bible as if it were documentary history and natural science, flat facts with no imagination or subtlety at all. Creation stories, flood stories, and conception/birth stories are often reduced to such a level, with the result that some people believe them literally and other people simply dismiss them as nonsense. In both cases what is missed is the religious meaning, the interior grace, that the sacred story has to convey.

In a mystery religion, there is always the outward sign and the interior meaning. The deep truths that the religion exists to make present and available cannot be said in ordinary words; they have to be hinted at, pointed to obliquely, symbolically imaged. Since what the religion reveals is about a reality that transcends our ordinary world, the means chosen for the revelation are frequently miracles. "Miracle" means that another dimension is operating: we are no longer talking about the facts of everyday life; we are pointing to something beyond.

Ronald Knox called the Eucharist a "window in the wall." All the sacraments and sacred stories and symbols of religion are such windows. It is the function of windows to be looked *through* rather than merely looked at. Edwin Bernbaum says that when we "recognize the symbol as a window and begin to look through it, . . . it turns transparent, loses its own features, and merges with what it reveals. At the end we cease even to see it as a window: it has become one with what it symbolizes. The view that it opened has transformed the symbol into an expression of reality itself"[1] (compare John 14:8–9).

So the first thing we need to do is to cultivate our sensitivity to the mystery aspect of the sacred materials that are presented to us. We need to be able to see the various levels of meaning in them, deeper and deeper and deeper. Nicodemus teaches us this. He knows that there is something mightily profound in what Jesus is about, and he wants to learn it, to be transformed by it. And so he tells Jesus that he understands that the works are "signs," that is, mysteries, external and visible embodiments of interior and invisible graces. And he knows that the graces come from God.

Born from Above

Jesus acknowledges that the signs are from God. He says to Nic-odemus, "Truly, truly, I tell you, except someone is born from above, he cannot see the kingdom of God" (John 3:3). Jesus himself does see the kingdom of God, and that is because he is "born from above" (John 3:13 and 13:3). This is an interesting expression, and since it bears directly on our concern about transformation, it will be helpful to look at it.

"From above" is *anōthen,* an adverb of place meaning also "from heaven." It has the root significance of being "above ground." It is the opposite of *katōthen* "from below." (Compare our "anode" and "cathode.") Both words can be made into nouns, *hoi anōthen,* "the living," those above ground, and *hoi katōthen,* "those in the nether world," the dead. Notice the relation to the sign of Baptism: the *going down* under the water, into the place beneath, and then the *coming up* above the water, into the place of the living. These words occur also in John 8:23, where Jesus says, "You are *ek tōn katō* [from, or of, or out of the things below], I am *ek tōn anō* [from the things above]." Here the meaning is "you are of this world, and I am not of this world but of the heavenly world."

The words also carry their reference to the living and the dead, frequent metaphors in the Gospels. For instance, Jesus advises the young man who was interested in following him but wanted first to bury his father (perhaps meaning to wait until after his father's death to take up the spiritual life), "Leave the dead [those who belong to and identify with this world] to bury their own dead; you [who feel the attraction of the heavenly world] come follow me" (Matt. 8:22). Jesus is himself the archetype of the living, as is made plain by the angel who speaks to the women who come to the tomb on Easter morning: "Why do you seek the Living One among the dead? He is not here" (Luke 24:5).

The transformation we are seeking is the passage from death to life. This is the central Christian mystery. Remember not to

take it merely literally — biologically or historically. The death
and life we are concerned with are spiritual; they have to do
with the interior and the invisible. In the First Epistle of John,
3:14, we read: "We know that we have passed out of death
into life, because we love the brethren. He who does not love
remains in death."

Nicodemus knows that what Jesus has just said to him
is a profoundly significant statement. Jesus began it with the
avouching words, "Amen, amen," indicating that what follows
is very important and that he has the authority to certify it.
Therefore Nicodemus knows that it has meaning on more than
one level, that no doubt it has layer after layer of significance.
Nicodemus asks that this deeper meaning be revealed to him.
He asks in an indirect and ironic way by identifying the obvious surface meaning, giving Jesus the opportunity to confide
the more secret meaning if he chooses to favor Nicodemus in
this way. "How can a man be born when he is old? Can he enter a second time into his mother's womb and be born?" But
even this apparently superficial interpretation of Jesus' words
has an ambiguity: the word for "a man" is *anthropos,* which
also means the human race, humanity at large. Nicodemus may
be understood as asking, "When humanity is already formed
and mature, can it somehow go back to its beginning and come
forth a second time from whatever cosmic womb originally gave
it birth?"

Jesus answers in the same solemn mode: "Truly, truly, I tell
you, unless anyone is born of water and the Spirit, he cannot
enter the kingdom of God. That which is born of the flesh is
flesh, and that which is born of the Spirit is spirit." This is the
same contrast we have already seen, between the above and the
below, between the living and the dead. It now appears as the
Spirit and the flesh. There is a merely human way of living,
represented here under the word "flesh," and then there is the
divine life, which comes from the Spirit.

Truth and Falsehood

We are still talking about transformation, the passage from the merely human and natural to the divine. It appears in yet another guise in the Gospel of John, the contrast between falsehood and truth. In the Last Discourse (John 14–17), Jesus promises to send the Holy Spirit, "the Spirit of truth" (John 16:13). In the conversation with Nicodemus, Jesus says that we must be "born of the Spirit." The Spirit will be our Parent. The Spirit of truth.

This makes us remember the text in which Jesus speaks of those who cannot receive his word as being "of your father the devil...a liar from the beginning...father of lies" (John 8:44). So the transformation is a passage from falsehood to truth. That is to say, what we wish to move away from is something that is actually rooted in falsehood; there is a mistake, an error, an untruth at its foundation. Getting rid of the belief in that falsehood is part of the movement from death to life.

The text of John 3:5 as we have it today reads "born of water and the Spirit." Scholars are uncertain whether "water" was actually mentioned by Jesus, whether the author of the Johannine text put it in, or whether the (ancient) editor of the text put it in to make a clear reference to the sacrament of Baptism. But since we are concerning ourselves with Baptism, let us accept it and see what it may mean.

This is not the first time the Bible mentions salvation by water and Spirit together. In Ezekiel (36:25) the Lord says, "I will sprinkle clean water upon you...a new heart will I give you and a new spirit will I put within you....I will put my spirit within you." In the noncanonical Book of Jubilees (1:23) these ideas are connected with the notion of the divine Parent: "I will create in them a holy spirit and I will cleanse them....I will be their Father and they shall be my children."

And in Jesus' own day the Qumran Essene community described how God would root out the spirit of falsehood from humanity:

Then God in his faithfulness [or by his truth] will purify all the works of man, and cleanse for himself the body of man, in order to consume every wicked spirit from the midst of his flesh, and to make him pure with [a] holy Spirit from every wicked deed; and he will sprinkle on him [a] spirit of truth like water for impurity...so as to give the righteous understanding in the knowledge of the Most High."[2]

Children of God

But the main theme and image for us is the divine Parent: "that which is born of the Spirit is spirit." "I will be their Father and they shall be my children." Being born of God is what Christianity is all about. In the Prologue to John's Gospel it is said of the mission of Jesus, in his core reality as the divine Word, "to those who received him he gave the power to become children of God" (1:12).

So Jesus says to Nicodemus, "Do not marvel because I told you you must be born from above." It is true that it is mysterious and hard to understand, but that doesn't keep it from being real. The wind blows and you can hear it, but you can't see it or tell where it comes from and where it is going; but there really is wind and it really is blowing. It is the same way with this birth from above: it really happens, although we can't give a complete account of it. At least this may be one way to read this part of the passage.

But when Jesus says, "So it is with every one who is born of the Spirit," perhaps he means that those who are born of the Spirit have no assignable origin or destination and are as free to do what they will as is the wind. The categories by which we measure and judge the things of the solid world do not apply to the world of the wind, and the categories of the world of the flesh do not apply to the world of the Spirit.

Children of God do not operate on the same principles as

do the children of this world. One could say that the whole of
Jesus' teaching is an elaboration on the theme of becoming children of God, a description of what that life is like. A good deal
of it is collected in one place in the Sermon on the Mount, which
opens with those great reversals we call the Beatitudes, in which
the states we usually consider to be accursed Jesus acclaims as
blessed. The Sermon goes on with a series of sayings beginning
"You have heard..." and completed by "but I say to you," in
which the principles of living accepted in the world are replaced
by principles of a much finer grade of moral discernment, principles that indeed come from quite a different perspective and
quite different assumptions about how reality is constructed and
what life is all about.

Take this text: "You have heard that it was said, You shall
love your neighbor and hate your enemy. But I say to you, Love
your enemies and pray for those who persecute you, so that you
may be children of your Father who is in heaven; for he makes
his sun rise on the evil and on the good, and sends rain on the
just and on the unjust.... You therefore must be perfect, as your
heavenly Father is perfect" (Matt. 5:43). That's the sort of thing
that is involved in becoming children of God. It obviously implies a totally different conception of the world and the purpose
of life from what we usually assume and usually act upon. Notice that our usual way divides the world into neighbors and
enemies, good and evil, just and unjust. But God is "perfect,"
that is, "complete," including all, excluding none. God is whole,
not cut into parts, not partial; God is one, not divided.

When we become children of God, we will be like that. Being "children of," or being "born from," are strong metaphors
for our relationship to God. They show a great intimacy, a great
likeness. They imply that the same life principle is present in us
as in God. That is what is meant by the image of "spirit" — literally, "breath." God breathes into us his own breath, and that
makes us live.

All this is included in the sacrament of Baptism: the passage
to a new kind of life, being born, in the waters of birth, from

God, and taking our first breath — after birth or after coming up from under the water — as the breath of God, the Spirit of God. This is the interior grace of which the external rite with water is the sign. You can appreciate that such a participation in the life of God is as truly impossible to comprehend with our words and concepts as is God himself. Thus it is something that is said, if it is said at all, as if with "closed lips."

Furthermore, it is a secret. But it is an "open secret." Indeed, Jesus preached it in public. But only those who have the ears to hear it are able to take it in. When the secret is told to us and we do receive it, we are "initiated"; we have "begun" our new life. This is the Easter mystery.

Exercises

This book will be most effective if used as a workbook or as an extended retreat. This means that actually *doing* the suggested exercises accompanying each chapter will help a great deal toward understanding and entering into the material of the next chapter. Therefore I recommend that you consider doing the following at this preliminary stage of the Lenten preparation for Easter.

1. Now, while there is still plenty of time, *plan* your Lent and Holy Week and Easter Week. Arrange to reserve at least half an hour a day for reflection and meditation on the last chapter you have read. Plan to attend Holy Week liturgies without domestic or social distractions. Leave yourself empty time on Thursday, Friday, and Saturday of Holy Week, as well as on Easter Sunday. Look ahead in the book and see that if you do the Stations of the Cross on Good Friday, it will take a while. And the whole sense of the emptiness and silence and Sabbath restfulness of Holy Saturday will be lost if there is a lot of bustling about getting ready for Easter the next day. Do not "let down" once we have come to Easter, but continue straight on, with the same faithfulness and energy you were willing to devote to Lent.

2. In particular, arrange to read "Prayer and Fasting" *before* Ash Wednesday, so that when you go to receive ashes and participate in the other services of this day, you will already be prepared. It is important to start your Lent well.

3. In the section on "Transformation," I discussed ways in which we identify ourselves. I suggested there that you "take pen and paper" and write down answers to the question, "Who am I?" This is a very useful exercise, a particularly important one for this book, because all the rest of the transformation strategy depends on our having a clear idea of our finite descriptions, our "earthly treasure." Rereading this section and writing down your description should be the first exercise. You may want to start a journal and keep notes of your thoughts and experiences as you go through the next weeks. You probably won't find all the descriptive words for yourself the first day; you can add to the list as you think of more items. Remember that the question will be whether you can release your identification in this way, so be especially careful to put down any designation that you feel you could not possibly give up (your "treasures"). You will get the most out of all these exercises if you keep these notes at hand and refer to them as you go along. As you feel you can release any of these identifications, you can mark them and see which ones you still have left.

4. Work with your list of descriptions prayerfully. Imagine Jesus saying to you, "I tell you, do not be anxious about your life, whether you are _____," and fill in the blank with whatever item you have in your list that you might be "anxious" about (such as whether you are rich, successful, married, beautiful, etc.). "Your life — your reality as a person — is far more than that, and God's love for you does not depend on such qualities. Feel secure in God's love, something you *can* rely on and not be anxious about."

If your descriptive item is one that you feel proud or complacent about ("I thank you, Lord, that I am not like other men"), then hear, "Do not presume that being _____ entitles you to privilege or praise. God is not moved or impressed by your being _____ [your 'treasures']. God loves you for yourself alone, quite apart from all these descriptions." Again, feel safe and affirmed without basing your secure feeling on being of the right religion or race or gender or whatever.

5. We are preparing to renew our Baptism at Easter. We want to be purified of all these unnecessary descriptions of ourselves by then. Believe that you can do this. Believe that God's love can be trusted to be unconditional. Don't put conditions on yourself for deserving your own esteem. If you rejoice in the reality of God's love for you, you will gradually free yourself of ego-protection behaviors and feelings, so you will spontaneously become a better person. It will happen naturally. Look forward to the work of purification as increasing relaxation and happiness.

6. Now I will propose a meditation exercise for you as an example of the kind of meditations you can set up for yourself hereafter. Since we are looking forward to Baptism, I suggest meditating on the Baptism of Jesus, because the basic principle of transformation will come out there. In the conversation with Nicodemus that we were just discussing, Nicodemus responds to Jesus' revelation of the divine birth from the Spirit by asking, "How shall this be?" It is reminiscent of the Virgin Mary saying to the angel Gabriel, "How shall this come about, that I can bring the Messiah into the world?" Gabriel had answered, "The Holy Spirit will come upon you." The same is true of us; we must be open to receive the Spirit. But how do we get "open"? Jesus' basic but brutal answer is, "You must die." That is, you must abandon your old principle of life and adopt a new one. That is what Baptism is all about.

Now accompany Jesus through his Baptism experience and its aftermath. Put yourself in his place and live through it all with him. Remember that Israel has been waiting and wondering for generations, "Where is our God?" "Why does God delay in ridding us of our oppressors?" "What *is* our relation to God?" "Have we misunderstood?" "Who are we?" "What is the meaning of our life?" Aren't these very like our own questions? Don't hesitate to feel the full force of the questions. That's what it means to *really ask.* Unless we do this, in a deep, existential, personal way, we will not come to true answers, the answers that are right for us, freeing for us. This is not a school exercise, in which the correct answer can be found in a book.

Your secret answer will be found only within *you.* St. Isaac of Nineveh (seventh century) advises:

> Make peace with yourself, and heaven and earth make peace with you. Take pains to enter your own innermost chamber and you will see the chamber of heaven, for they are one and the same, and in entering one you behold them both. The stairway to the kingdom is within you, secret in your soul. Cast off the burden of sin and you will find within you the upward path that will make your ascent possible.[3]

Into this context comes John the Baptist, preaching that God is coming and we must get ready for him; we must "prepare the way of the Lord." And he baptizes people as a sign of repentance and preparation for the Lord's coming.

Jesus comes to this scene: John in the River Jordan, preaching and baptizing. Jesus identifies with all of us, with our questions, with our questing. We, in our meditation, join with him in deeply feeling the questions, the seeking.

Jesus enters the water and is baptized by John. And as he comes up out of the water, he has a transforming experience. It seems as though suddenly the heavens open to him and the Holy Spirit descends upon him as gently as a dove, and he hears a voice saying, "You are my beloved child, in whom I am well pleased." The experience is so overwhelming that he is "driven by the Spirit into the wilderness," where he remains, fasting, for forty days.

I make this suggestion about this mystery-event: Jesus has heard the words, "You are my beloved child, in whom I am well pleased." During the long fast in the desert he meditates on these words, letting them sink into his consciousness until he

deeply and truly knows that they are real and true and knows
what they mean. What we have to realize is that these same
words are said to us. As Jesus carried our questions and seeking into the river, by virtue of his intention to identify with even
the least of us, so he receives the answer for us. We, too, in our
deepest reality, are beloved children of God. Therefore, we also
have to go into the desert and fast and meditate deeply on the
truth and meaning of the divine words.

Jesus sorted through the various possible implications of the
words. Some interpretations he rejected; these are represented
in the story of the Three Temptations. The temptations all begin, "If you are the Son of God, then...." But Jesus puts these
possible meanings aside as unworthy of one born of God.

More important for us are the meanings that he accepted and
that are apparent in his subsequent teaching and actions. But
even so, we still have to do our own meditating and sorting.
What are the consequences for *me* if I am really born of God?
What could that possibly mean? What are the temptations for
me? What aspects of my present life would have to "die"? What
am I taking for granted that I should question and reject? Jesus
says that God doesn't prefer some to others, and that we too —
if we are to be "perfect" like our divine Parent — must give
up dividing and preferring, identifying with some and excluding
others. How am I doing that? If I am indeed a child of God, do
I need to cling to this or that image of myself in terms of favorable or unfavorable qualities? Do I want to gain enough security
through believing in the revelation to feel free to drop some of
the ideas and attitudes that I have been using to "protect" my
life? Can I hear the divine voice of the baptismal experience and
let go and enter the transformation?

The exercise for us is to identify the assumptions and the
practices in our lives that need to be left behind, that must
be abandoned. Especially we need to look for the *general
principles,* the notions and values that we have been taking
for granted that support all the practices that we see to be
insufficient for the divine life.

We may be good at loving our friends but weak at loving
our enemies. What's the principle involved? The principle is that
there is a difference between friends and enemies: friends do us
good; enemies do us harm. "Love" is an attitude we have toward what is helpful or pleasant to us; "hate" is an attitude we
have toward what is harmful or painful to us. This is a principle
on which we are probably organizing our lives to a greater or
lesser degree.

The reason we need to search for the general principle, the
fundamental falsehood, is that we want to get the *root* out —
"Lay the axe to the root of the tree," as John the Baptist said
(Matt. 3:10). Otherwise, the same falsehood we remove in one
instance will show up again in another case.

You won't settle all this in one meditation. This is only an orientation meditation for the whole course of these exercises. At
this point, after going through these reflections, you need only
decide whether you are ready to take seriously a search into the
"innermost chamber" and to make the exertions necessary to
give the transformation a chance.

It will make a big difference in what you gain from interacting with this book if you will actually perform the meditations
and follow out the other exercises. You will read each suc-
ceeding chapter with a mind that has grown through your
meditations, and therefore what arises in your mind on the occasion of reading these words will be different from what you
would have understood if you simply read the book straight
through out of curiosity. The desired gain is not that you should
find out what I think, but that somehow provoked by this reading (to interest, disagreement, or some creative side-step), you
should enter into your own depths and discover your own truth.

— Two —

PRAYER AND FASTING

⌘

L ENT IS THE SEASON of preparation for the high mysteries of Easter. In the ancient church, and in many churches today, it is the time of special training and instruction of the catechumens who are to be baptized during the Easter Vigil. Many of us will renew our baptismal vows during that ceremony, and we have all of Lent — we need all of Lent — to get ready for this important experience in which we deepen our transformation, the transformation symbolized as death and resurrection.

The Twin Disciplines

The church recommends to us two practices for our Lenten observance: prayer and fasting. They are twin disciplines. They help each other, as I hope to show presently. But what do we mean when we say that they are "disciplines"? Two meanings of "discipline" seem to me to apply: one is drawn from athletic training and means to gain strength and skill and control by regular living, care for one's health, and persistent practice. The other is drawn more from the root of the word and means a teaching, with respect to which one is a "disciple," or student under a "doctor," a teacher of a "doctrine."

Jesus invites us to become his disciples and to learn from him by imitating, copying, and following him, by doing his works:

30

> The one who abides in me, and in whom I abide, is the one who bears much fruit, for apart from me you can do nothing. . . . But if you do abide in me, and my words abide in you, then you may ask whatever you will, and it shall be done for you. By this my Father is glorified, that you bear much fruit, and so prove to be my disciples. (John 15:5, 7–8)

And St. Paul urges us to practice athletic discipline: "Every athlete exercises self-control in all things. They do it for a perishable wreath, but we for an imperishable one" (1 Cor. 9:25).

Both Jesus and Paul are talking about real experience, true newness of life that we can begin to experience even now. When we fast, we do gain skill and control over ourselves, and we also learn many things. When, in prayer, we attend to Jesus as Teacher, we learn all that is necessary to our salvation; and when, following him, we put these teachings into practice, we become skillful in life and blessed.

Of course, no learning or training is quick or easy. But it's worth the exertion. The author of the Letter to the Hebrews says:

> For the moment all discipline seems painful rather than pleasant; later it yields the peaceful fruit of righteousness to those who have been trained by it. Therefore, lift your drooping hands and strengthen your weak knees, and make straight paths for your feet. (Heb. 12:11–13A)

> Let us also lay aside every weight, and sin which clings so closely, and let us run with perseverance the race that is set before us, looking to Jesus the pioneer and perfecter of our faith, who for the joy that was set before him endured the cross, despising the shame, and is seated at the right hand of the throne of God. (Heb. 1B–2)

That's a powerful exhortation, and one feels that we ought to respond to it with enthusiasm. The same writer says, at the beginning of that twelfth chapter, that we are "surrounded by a great cloud of witnesses," people who can testify that they have gone this way, practiced the disciplines, and gained the blessings. They've had the experience.

They all tell us, however, that merely "believing in" their experiences won't do us much good — though it can get us started and inspire us with confidence; we must ourselves do what those people did and have our own experiences and become witnesses in our turn, able to say, "Those who have gone before us on this path have not deceived us; it *is* worth the exertion — in fact, the effort is as nothing compared with the reward."

The expression "prayer and fasting" comes to us from the Gospel story of the healing of the epileptic boy in Mark 9:29. The context is that the boy was possessed by an evil spirit, which Jesus cast out. His disciples asked why they had not been able to cast it out, and Jesus, after first attributing their failure to their lack of faith, adds that "this kind cannot be driven out by anything but prayer and fasting."

This verse is probably a gloss on the original text, indicating that several generations of practicing Christians had discovered by experience that some parts of our transformation have to be dealt with in this way. This is reassuring to the rest of us. In the first place, we know that others have had the same difficulties as ourselves; what we are experiencing in our struggles is "par for the course." Second, we know that, from the teaching of Jesus on down through the lines of disciples, people have found remedies, have discovered ways that work, and have passed them on in the tradition to each generation of neophytes. Finally, this reminds us that from us, to whom much has been given from the past and the disciple/teachers who have preceded us, much will be expected. We must train and practice, believe and pray, and come into original experience ourselves, so that we in turn can become teachers and resource persons for those who come after us.

"Evil spirits" — errors in our ways of thinking and hurtful forms of feeling — have to be eradicated, and the Holy Spirit, God's personal presence, has to be allowed to enter and fill us and make us live. It is for this that our ancestors recommend to us the practice of prayer and fasting. And this means for us liberation and happiness, a sense of meaning and satisfaction in our lives. We are not fasting as a way of punishing ourselves, expressing our sense of guilt, blaming ourselves. Quite the contrary. Once we have corrected those faults that lie within our (present) power to correct, we will actually fast from feeling any guilt. For in many cases it is the accumulation of such negative feelings that builds up a "spirit of evil" in our lives and that must be cast out.

Prayer will enable us to release the "evil spirits" in ourselves, and deeper fasting — from erroneous thought patterns discovered through prayer — will enable us to drop faults that were not in the beginning under our conscious control.

Baptismal Promises: Renounce and Embrace

But now let's look at the baptismal promises. These will vary in form according to denomination, but in general the promises are partly renunciations and partly commitments, a negative way and an affirmative way. I think that we may say, as a kind of format for our Lenten work, that the negative way of renunciation relates to fasting and the affirmative way of commitment relates to prayer. They are two types of experience, two ways of preparation for Easter Baptism.

Looking at the promises, we see that some of them are ancient, for instance, that we promise to "love our neighbors as ourselves," and some of them seem to be of more recent origin, such as the Book of Common Prayer's vow to "strive for justice and peace among all people" and to "respect the dignity of every human being." We say that we "believe in" these ideals, and we give lip service to them readily enough, but when we work out their implications — and their applications — we often run into surprises and difficulties.

What if striving for justice and peace among all people were

to involve for Americans that we use no more than our fair
share of the wealth and resources of the earth? and possibly
even be willing to share job markets with poor people in other
countries? On an individual level, does loving my neighbor as
myself — as much as myself, even perhaps as a kind of extension
of myself so that whatever happens to the least of my neighbors
I regard as happening to me — does this kind of love mean that
I am not to be resentful when my competitor gets the account
or the job or the market that I had hoped I would get? Does it
mean that maybe I should even have some sympathy with the
competitor and rejoice? And on a very personal level, if I am to
respect the dignity of every human being, does that imply that
I must forego making demeaning and slighting remarks, put-
downs, either directly to people or behind their backs? A little
experience with trying to put these ideals into practice reveals
that there is quite a lot of Satan-renouncing to be done and that
some of these evil spirits are rather tough to dislodge.

One of our worst demons doesn't at first look like what we
usually think of as a demon. We may even associate it with a
kind of virtue. This is the flip side of the demeaning remarks we
may be tempted to make about other people, namely, the negative self-talk that so many of us engage in. It takes two main
forms. The first is believing that I don't measure up somehow to
what is praiseworthy and to be respected and admired and that
therefore my essential value as a person is diminished. Almost
always these hurtful beliefs and feelings have been imposed on
us by other people around us who have treated us disrespect-
fully, and if our detractors have been powerful enough, we
will probably have coped by buying into their image of us and
thinking of ourselves as deficient.

It is my belief that this is a well-nigh universal malady and
very difficult to get over. Nevertheless, it is an error and a failure to keep the baptismal promise to "respect the dignity of
every human being." The first human being to whom that duty
is due is oneself. We have no proper foundation for loving and
respecting our neighbors if we do not do this first.

We are assured that God values each of us infinitely and makes no comparisons among us, and we are not to be lured into believing that our value is established in any other way. This is told us over and over, and it is displayed to us by the stories Jesus tells and by his own behavior. It is very important, indeed essential, that we believe this, really take it in and absorb it, because this is the faith that liberates us, that is victorious over what the world would have us believe (1 John 5:4), the faith-realization that sets us free from our inner "spirits of evil" and opens us to the heavenly life.

The Christian expectation is that this heavenly life is to take flesh in the world and the world is to be transformed by it. The liberation Jesus brings is to be incarnated in every aspect of our lives and is to spread from the realization in our minds and hearts to our social and economic lives as we faith-fully continue the struggle for justice that has to complete the full stature of Christ.

This brings us to the second form that negative self-talk takes, namely, saying — when we face something that we might reasonably expect to do — "Oh, I can't do that." "It's too hard." "I'm not good at that." "I don't have the skill (or discipline, will-power, patience, whatever)." This claimed helplessness, claimed impotence, is a great impediment to our spiritual growth.

But the baptismal promises give us the key. When we are asked to commit ourselves to the Christian life, to believe and to practice according to the revelation, we are encouraged to say, "I will, with God's help." We can acknowledge that a great demand is being made on us, even that we might not dare to undertake it relying on our own power alone. But because we trust in divine support, have firm confidence that God will enable us to fulfill those ideals that have been set before us, we do not hesitate to embrace it.

In the context of building up the Body of Christ by working for justice in the world, we can apply this confidence to a willingness to persevere without giving up either our action or our hope or our good humor. And in the context of the Lenten observance that strengthens us for such struggles, we can apply this to the whole course of progressing on the path of transformation.

We are all called to be saints, and we can become so with God's help. "This is the will of God, your sanctification," says the Apostle Paul (1 Thess. 4:3). We are going to undertake various forms of fasting and praying. We have no call to feel incompetent or weak, to shrink back and say "I can't." We are entitled to say boldly, "I will, with God's help."

Fasting for Freedom

Most Christians are familiar with the idea of "giving up something" for Lent. In my early days in the church, back in the 1950s when I was twenty-something and having a great time studying philosophy at Fordham University and teaching third grade in a parochial school in the Bronx, the students — both the little kids and the adults — would ask each other, "What are you giving up for Lent this year?" Some of my third-graders were quite cunning about it: they proposed to give up school! One of the Jesuits at the university gave up cigarettes one year, and it took all the support his friends and relatives could give him to get him through it, but he made it. Mark Twain, you may remember, said that he was always careful to have at least one vice in reserve, so that when it came time to give up something, he'd have a candidate handy!

The first year I was in the church, my spiritual director, a life-loving Italian, looking at me probably through his mama's eyes, saw right away that what I needed was fattening up. So, having implored me to eat more pasta, he assigned me to make the Stations of the Cross every day instead of doing without calories. I remember the first time I set out to do this, in the university church, where the Stations are represented by large bas-reliefs. I came to the First Station, "Jesus Is Condemned to Death," and it hit me that I was contemplating my own spiritual journey. "Good grief," I said to myself. "What have I gotten myself into?"

But it shouldn't have come as such a surprise. Even Socrates had said, plainly enough, that the life-path of the philosopher is practicing every day to die. Both Socrates and Jesus explained, in various ways, that this dying, as a spiritual path, meant fasting from what we take to be our dependencies in this world. That was the first lesson that Jesus brought us from his own experience of fasting: "We do not live by bread alone, but by every word that comes from the mouth of God." And both Jesus and Socrates told us repeatedly that such fasting really means freedom. When fasting is done correctly, it is not a hurting but a healing. We are not diminished; rather, we expand. Life is made richer, not poorer. *The heart of fasting is being freed from the belief that we are dependent on the many sorts of "bread" that we have hitherto thought that we could not do without.*

The corollary of this is that fasting, properly speaking, hasn't really happened until the dependency — the belief and the experience that we can't do without — has died in our minds. If we go on clinging in our memories and imaginations to what we have outwardly given up, we are not yet free.

There is an amusing Buddhist story about two monks who are journeying on foot from one village to another. They come to a river that has to be forded, and there they find a young woman in a nice new garment, obviously reluctant to wade through the muddy water. The older of the monks offers to carry her across, and she gratefully accepts. The two monks walk on by themselves in silence, for maybe a mile or so, and then the younger one, who has been brooding all the while, suddenly bursts out, "How could you have touched that woman? You have violated your monastic vows and defiled your robe of renunciation!" The older monk looks up, surprised, and says mildly, "Are you still carrying that girl? I put her down on the bank of the river."

It isn't the deprivation that is useful in fasting — as if we should keep the desire yet deny ourselves the enjoyment of what we desire. That produces only frustration, not freedom. No, fasting is intended to release us gently from the various bondages we're caught up in, so that we can realize in our personal experience that we do actually live by God and that we don't have to insist on having this or that in the way of worldly goods or positions of advantage. It is a way of gradually appreciating that although the forms of this life will eventually pass away — return to dust, as we are reminded on Ash Wednesday — the life that we still will live, we will live to God (Rom. 6:10).

Fasting releases spiritual power in us. But it has to be joined to prayer. In the following lessons I will develop deeper and more subtle forms of both prayer and fasting. I mentioned the negative thinking and the empowering response of faith here at the very beginning because I believe they are central concerns to the whole exercise and we need to be alerted to them from the start so that we can be working on them the whole time.

But the particular fasting for beginning Lent is ordinary fasting, as it affects nonessential food and drink, smoking, recreation — whatever in our opinion we would be better off without but that we feel would be hard to give up. What it is depends on our individual case; it is our particular pet "addiction," something we feel helpless with respect to, something that has some kind of hold on us. Remember that freedom is the goal.

We need to take time at this point to choose what we will undertake to free ourselves from and to make up our minds that we are going to be serious enough about it that we can make the corresponding meditations from a real, existential point of view, facing something actual and concrete in our lives. Then we will apply ourselves to gaining a sense of power in this situation by the practice of mental prayer.

Mental Prayer

Mental prayer is distinguished from formal and vocal prayer, prayers of set forms of words that are spoken. Also, it is prayer that is not concerned with presenting petitions to God, or even primarily thanksgiving or praise. It is directed more, you might say, to cultivating a friendship with God, a love relationship, moving toward the enormously liberating and empowering realization of our divine filiation, the truth that we are children — offspring, descendents — of God, heirs of the divine nature and power.

I am going to describe a particular method that I think covers several modes of prayer and that is easily accessible to everyone. It is perfectly simple in its beginning but it leads on to deeper levels, some of which we will discuss in the chapters ahead.

In this prayer, you hold still for some time, probably about thirty minutes. So a suitable place needs to be chosen where you will not be disturbed. Different prayer postures can be assumed, generally kneeling or sitting.

Sitting may be on a straight, firm chair or on the floor. If you sit on the floor without an elevating cushion, you will want a wall at your back. If you sit without back support, you may prefer a firm cushion, about eight to ten inches high and a foot in diameter; you position the tip of the spine only two or three inches from the front edge of the cushion so that you are leaning against it more than actually sitting on it.

The legs can then be folded in various ways according to the flexibility of the limbs, the harder positions being those that place one or both feet on top of the thighs rather than under them. Find a posture that is comfortable enough to maintain and attentive enough to signify respect and prevent drowsiness. Some experimentation may be necessary. The elevated cushion should make it possible for the knees of the folded legs to go down to the floor, so that you are balanced on two knees and the tip of the spine.

If you choose kneeling, you will want either a support in

front of you or a kneeling bench under you that holds the body up at a slight angle and prevents its weight from resting on the feet and lower legs, which are tucked under the bench. You can also shift from upright kneeling to sitting — on your heels or on a bench (as in church) and back again, as the character of the prayer suggests.

In all postures the back, neck, and head are to be kept straight up, except when making a bow. The eyes may be closed, loosely focused on the floor about a yard ahead, or in church fastened on a significant object — Bible, cross, tabernacle, ikon. The attention is to be guarded and directed to the prayer with full interest and feeling.

You start with a Gospel story in which Jesus does something in which you can participate. The prayer focuses on the presence of Jesus, who is God as human and therefore readily accessible to us human beings. But, having connected with him in his humanity, we can then "travel on" him, since he says that he is the Way, the Road (John 14:6). We can try to enter into his mind, to see the world that he sees and to think about it the way he does and to feel toward it the way he feels. Pressing further, we can try to sense the general tenor of his life, his sense of himself. In this way, we come to Jesus as the truth and as the life, and we become able to pray as he prays. That is the overall pattern of the prayer I will propose throughout these exercises, but it begins with the simple way of entering into a story.

Several stories come to my mind when I think of the resistance we feel when we consider resolving to release one of our dependencies and when I remember the power from above that is implied in the way the church has us make our commitments to transformation: "I will, with God's help." The first story is John 5:2–9, the case of the man lying beside the miraculous pool, who has been ill or disabled for thirty-eight years. Read the story first; then take up your preferred prayer posture and imagine the scene vividly, applying all the senses. See the whole landscape in color, get a sense of the spaces involved, see close up what the people look like. Hear all the sounds, not only the words spoken by the principal characters but the background noises. If you're imaginative enough — and brave enough! — you might try to imagine the smells. If the story involves your eating something, taste it. If you touch something or someone, or are touched, feel it.

First, go through the story as if you are an unknown observer, as if it is being played on a stage. This way you get a first feel for the various characters and their points of view. Then go through the story again, this time as one of the characters. You may choose to be one of the minor characters. For instance, in this story of the man disabled for thirty-eight years, you may be one of the crowd or another invalid lying by the pool or a disciple of Jesus. This way you get a little closer to Jesus, depending on how you situate yourself. Can you see him, hear him, clearly? What do you think is going on when the crucial moment comes, when Jesus asks the man, "Do you want to be healed?" Do you understand the man to answer yes? Or no? Or "I can't"?

A Real Friend

That's the warm-up. Now you are ready to go through the whole thing again, but this time you will be the man who has lain by this pool so long without relief. In putting yourself in his place, consider that his disability is actually your dependency that you are considering trying to give up for Lent. Has it disabled you? Maybe for quite a long time? And like the man in the story, have you made your adjustments, worked out a lifestyle that includes and accommodates your dependency, perhaps even built your life around it, whatever it is, this something that you think you cannot do without? And have you combined an attitude of "Of course I'd like to be cured" with "But it can't be done"?

Now, from your position by the pool, you see Jesus approach. At first he seems to be just strolling up to the pool, but after a bit you notice that he is coming in your direction, and finally you are convinced that he is heading directly toward you. How does he look? How does he look at you? What's it like to be that near him? What do you feel? What does he say? Maybe he asks your name, how long you've been here, what's the matter with you. A little friendly chitchat, showing interest, caring.

Something about him perhaps makes you feel like confiding in him. You're not inclined to give him a merely polite reply as you usually do when someone asks, "How are you?" Also, you feel that somehow you can't tell him anything but the truth. It's as though he can see into you. But that's okay. He's not a faultfinder; he's a comforting presence. You begin to feel that he could be a real friend.

He knows you have troubles, but it's as though he sees past all that and really appreciates you as you are deep down. That's wonderfully helpful, just that. As he talks with you, your confidence in him starts to take a new turn. The way he enables you to feel yourself in some new deeper spot and the way he talks from some deep central place in himself — even though you're saying fairly ordinary things to one another — is not like the usual superficial conversation. You sense that there's some extra kind of life in him and that somehow it overflows onto — into — anyone who pays attention and is open. You start to hope that maybe here is somebody who can help you.

And then he turns and asks you very earnestly, "Do you want to be healed?" The question seems to go deep, deep down into your consciousness, and now it's a real question, because... because if you say yes, something miraculous might happen, you might actually be healed. It had always been safe enough before to say, "Of course I want to be healed," because you didn't take seriously the possibility of really changing. But now he seems to be inviting you to face the reality of being free of whatever has disabled you. And that would change your whole life. Are you ready to cope with that? Even if it's a small thing, the fact that you could change, could pass from having to have it to being free of it, would mean that you are not so helpless after all, you do have the capacity to be other than you are. That means the door is open to greater changes. All sorts of other dependencies might depart, following this one. Where would it end? What would it mean?

Now having gotten to this point in the prayer, stay there for some time, just focusing on that moment in which Jesus asks his dangerous question. I can't tell you what to do after that; it depends on what you answer and what he then says or does. That will emerge in your own prayer. But the theme is that Jesus is a real helper. You are not alone. You are not trapped in a situation about which nothing can be done. Jesus helps by being what he is, by giving his full attention to the real you, a you that is deeper and stronger than you had known, and by believing in you, by having confidence in you.

He asks you a simple question, which seems to have an obvious answer and seems to carry with it the implication that he will maybe do something for you — but perhaps what you feel is that he has already done it, just by being with you and asking his question. Perhaps you know that when you answer the question by saying yes, and really meaning it with all that it entails, you will already be healed. And so it will be only natural for him to say, "Then, since you are free, you might as well get up and walk."

Exercises

This is an example of the type of prayer we may call dialogue prayer, in which we talk back and forth with Jesus, but in which we are building up a strong sense of his presence and gradually discovering a new sense of our own reality. To get the most out of this lesson series, you should experiment with this prayer during the next few days, before reading further. Here are some more stories that you can use:

Matthew 9:27–30: Here our dependency is represented as

something that hampers us by preventing us from seeing life truly and seeing where our value is really lodged. We believe that we can't be happy or comfortable or fulfilled without such-and-such. But now we at least suspect that that's not the whole story and that perhaps we would actually have a fuller life if we found that we could live without such-and-such after all.

Luke 13:10–13: Be the woman who is limited by an oppression that doesn't allow her to stand up straight. Notice that Jesus calls you because he wants to release you. Hear his words of freedom and feel his hands on you, lifting you. Linger in that moment.

Mark 3:1–5 (Luke 6:6–10): Be the man whose hand (faculty of action) is withered. Consider how you could be freer to act if your fasting is successful. Again, feel the power in Jesus to help, his desire to do so, his confidence in you when he tells you to stretch forth your hand — the hand that you thought couldn't move. Stay with this empowering command of his and the feeling of new life and ability.

Invite Jesus into your own scenes, visualize him in your home, your workplace; talk to him about your life; listen and watch carefully to see how he responds. He "speaks to" you through your own deeper self, for he "dwells in" you (see John 14:7, 20, 23, 26; 16:13). The purer the sincerity of your asking, the wiser the answer you will receive, often quite surprising.

Theological Postscript: Ash Wednesday

Something very important is said to us on Ash Wednesday, at the very beginning of our preparation for the Easter mysteries, which we cannot properly appreciate until after we have passed through the mysteries. Nevertheless, because it indicates the course of the whole movement, it must be said here and the meaning pointed to.

In the liturgical churches ash is prepared by burning the palm leaves of the previous year's Palm Sunday. A small smudge of this ash is applied to the foreheads of those undertaking the Lenten discipline, together with these words: "Remember, human being, that you are dust, and unto dust you shall return."

We human beings are indeed made of "dust" — star dust — as is everything else in this universe. The cells of our bodies, including our senses and brains, through whose help we know and think about these things, are composed of molecules made of atoms whose complex nuclei were fused together in the fiery hearts of exploding stars. This scattered "dust" was rolled up by a new star, sucked by its gravitational power into a great swirl that would settle out as a central sun surrounded by a family of planets. In our system, one planet, Earth, having all the right conditions, gradually organized the star dust of which it was made into very complicated molecules and then living beings.

The living beings are a traffic of molecules, constantly coming and going, forms building up and forms coming apart. We know that in our own bodies cells are always dying and being discarded while new ones are coming into being. "Living" is the name for this traffic, this constant motion, this coming and going, this building and destroying, this birthing and dying. The human body is always being built up from the dust (plants and animals that we eat are in turn made of minerals, water, atmospheric gases — Earth itself) and is always reverting to dust. You can actually see this dust, drawn out of your mattress by a vacuum cleaner, the same fine white ash that a cremated body is reduced to. The situation is not so simple as being born once and dying once. Coming to be and passing away are going on all the time.

Notice, too, that the appearance of the human body changes greatly from infancy to maturity to old age. So it must be in the process of changing in this way at every moment, even though we become aware of the change only when we compare times sufficiently far apart.

Human being, this is what you are: this process, this constant changing, this traffic. But, then, what is it in me that seems to be the same? Good question. If you will investigate what you call your "personality," you will find that it changes too. In fact, "personality" is also a "traffic," nothing but relations with other personally charged beings in our world. Not only does nothing in our body or personality *remain* without changing; nothing about either of them *is* anything *in itself*. They are both entirely made up of relations with other beings like themselves.

But I continue to feel that there is something in me — that which is really *I*, that which says "I AM" before I add the adjectives describing the relations of my body or personality, something that has unity and continuity and selfhood. What is that? Now we grasp the question. Is there an answer in Ecclesiastes 12:7? "The dust returns to the earth as it was, and the spirit returns to God who gave it." Is the "daily dying" that I mentioned earlier in connection with Socrates and that St. Paul also speaks of (1 Cor. 15:31) a work of sorting out the "dust" from the "spirit"? And of realizing that I AM the spirit in a different way than I am the dust?

These are hard questions, and we are trying to work up to the place where we can deal with them more directly, but it may be good to know from the start that this is the kind of thing that the Easter mysteries exist to enable us to discover by our own direct experience. Direct experience is the key. I believe there is another important clue in 1 Corinthians 2:9–16.

It is written,

> "What no eye has seen, nor ear heard,
> nor the heart of man conceived,
> what God has prepared for those who love him,"

[this] God has revealed to us through the Spirit. For the Spirit searches everything, even the depths of God. For what person knows a man's thoughts except the spirit of

the man which is in him? So also no one comprehends the thoughts of God except the Spirit of God.

Now we have received not the spirit of the world, but the Spirit which is from God, that we might understand the gifts bestowed on us by God.

And we impart this in words not taught by human wisdom but taught by the Spirit, interpreting spiritual truths to those who possess the Spirit.

The merely natural man does not receive the gifts of the Spirit of God, for they are folly to him, and he is not able to understand them because they [must be] spiritually discerned.... But we have the mind of Christ.

I call attention to "the merely natural man" and suggest that this is the human being made of dust. And I call attention to the claim that we have received the Spirit of God that "searches everything, even the depths of God," in a way somehow parallel to the way we know our own depths. Finally I point to the teaching that the gifts of the Spirit of God (compare Ecclesiastes: our spirit itself is the chief gift of God) must be "spiritually discerned" (not "taught by human wisdom"), and this can be done because "we have the mind of Christ."

To try to understand our situation-in-reality from the outside, by a kind of object-oriented observation, is to use "human wisdom"; it results merely in the conclusion that human beings are made of dust and will dissolve into dust. We need to grasp our reality from the inside, by *being* our reality rather than trying to look at it, by coinciding with it subjectively, by an "existential understanding."[1] This is why it is so important to do the exercises as we go along, because many of these things must be "spiritually discerned," that is, personally and existentially experienced for oneself. Otherwise they will not make sense; they will be "folly." "Spiritual truths" make sense only when interiorly experienced as one's own being, in one's own spirit. Eyes and ears cannot relate to spiritual truths, and even concepts can only point to them. But they are "revealed to us through the Spirit," that is, in "existential understanding."

All the exercises, the fastings and the meditations, are intended to provoke such personal experience, to lead us deeper and deeper into "the spirit" where the divine revelations will make more and more sense and the transformation will go forward.

— *Three* —

OUR SECRET SELF

═══════════════════ ᥴ ═══════════════════

E ASTER is about transformation. This transformation is symbolically, mythically, sacramentally, imaged as death/ resurrection, in turn imaged as Baptism. We are trying to undergo the transformation by experiencing the sacramental power of these images. We are following Jesus as our archetype, as well as our teacher and our friend, the one who exemplifies the very transformation we are facing. He is also what is called in Greek the *mystagōgos,* the mystagogue, the one who leads us into the mysteries, the one who initiates us into the secret, into that which is told with closed lips. And he is himself the Way into which he leads us, as he is the Life into which we are led.

Therefore we are doing two parallel things, or one thing that can be approached in two ways: we are going deeply into ourselves, dying to our former way of seeing, feeling, thinking, acting, in order to discover our secret self and be reborn into a new way of seeing, feeling, thinking, acting; and we are going deeply into Jesus, the exemplar, as he invites us deeper and deeper into himself as the Living Way.

This discovery of the secret self is central to spiritual life, and our practice of fasting is directed to facilitating it. As Jesus said, it's a matter of finding that we do not live by bread alone but by the life of God. The usefulness of these abstinences that we perform during Lent — which sometimes appear trivial — is that in some curious way they awaken strange places in our consciousness and oblige us to rearrange our conscious energies, reorder

49

the way our wants and satisfactions are organized. That can be quite revealing. What do we really want out of life? What is our conception of what life is all about?

An Appetite for the Infinite

A friend of mine in New York, a philosophy professor, is fond of getting into philosophical discussions with taxi drivers. He has a favorite story he likes to tell. It begins with the cabdriver showing an inclination to talk about himself, and so my friend, Norrie, asks, "Are you happy?" No, says the cabbie, too many problems. "What would make you happy?" "Give me a million dollars, and I'd have it made." "All right. Let's suppose you have the million dollars. What will you do?" He said he would pay off all his debts. "Fine, they're paid. Now what?" "Well, I'd buy a house. Maybe two or three houses, in different climates." "Good. Now what?" "I'd want a wife. As long as we're fantasizing, I'll take several — let's say in different cities, and I could travel around to them." "Done. Now what?" Then he proposed to travel, to indulge his hobbies, to see and do things he'd always dreamed of and each time Norrie agreed: "Granted. What more?"

After a while the driver began to quiet down. Then he suddenly turned around, right in the middle of a crowded avenue, giving my poor friend quite a fright, and said, "Say, there's something funny going on here. I can't seem to get to the bottom of all this. What am I really looking for, after all?" At that point the philosopher had him hooked and was able to show him that the human being has an unlimited capacity for the good, for happiness — or better, we have a capacity for the Infinite, for nothing finite satisfies us. No matter how much we have, we don't feel that this is it; we want to go on.[1]

But what kind of being is it that has a capacity for, an appetite for, the Infinite? We don't yet know our secret self. We don't yet know our heart's desire. Prayer and fasting help us find them.

The Prayer of Jesus

How did Jesus pray? I can't pretend to answer that, but I can share some of my meditations stimulated by this question and invite you to develop your own.

The particular idea I want to develop here is that the foundation of Jesus' prayer was his sense of his divine Father dwelling in him. He knows that he "abides" in his Father's love (John 15:10). This is, of course, the key to everything, and this is where we should take the greatest care to follow him. He explicitly promises us that the Father loves us even as the Father loves him and that he himself loves us as the Father loves him (John 14:23, 15:9, 17:26).

What enables him to be so sure? We might answer that he has had powerful religious experiences; he has heard the Father actually speak to him. And besides, he himself is God the Son incarnate and might be expected to remember that fact, even through the thick veil of his human nature. But the important point for us is that he does not claim privilege in this respect, but clearly intends that we should have the same experiences, the same certainty that he himself has. "The Father himself loves you," he urges, and will make his home with you (John 16:26, 14:23). Jesus has shared everything he has received from the Father: "All I have heard from my Father I have made known to you" (John 15:15), and "when the Spirit of truth comes, he will guide you into all the truth" (John 16:13). "The glory which [the Father] has given me, I have given [you]" (John 17:22).

So let us look for suggestions as to how we can follow him into this sureness that God is present in and with us. Jesus can be paraphrased as saying, "Come to me, all of you who work so hard and are so heavily burdened, and I will show you how to obtain relief. For I am meek and lowly of heart — this is the way to find rest and peace for your souls" (Matt. 11:28).

We aren't generally very attracted to the idea of being "meek and lowly of heart." It doesn't agree with our ambitions to claim our dignity, demand respect, and enforce our will on people and circumstances around us. But why do we want to do such things? Jesus might ask us. Why have such ambitions? Has fulfilling them ever brought anyone happiness? Indeed, has anyone ever succeeded in fulfilling them to his or her satisfaction?

The answer to this question is no. These are unrealistic ambitions, based on falsehood. They bring only disquiet of spirit, not happiness. They do not constitute the deep desire of our secret heart. Taking them seriously shows a superficial, short-sighted, immature, and self-defeating attitude toward life. Strong words, we might say. Just so, Jesus might reply. But if you want to be free, you've got to get to the truth (John 8:32).

"Meek and Lowly"

Let me tell you a little more about being "meek and lowly of heart." It isn't what you were thinking. "Meek," even in English, means something strong, not something weak. My etymological dictionary says that it means "gentle, kind, free from pride and self-will." As such, I say, it is the basis of the ideal of the "gentleman." Only those who are very strong and sure in themselves can be gentle. The insecure tend to bluster, to attack, to try to cut others down so that they may stand taller. Those who are really tall, strong, and confident don't engage in such weak behavior. They have the resources to be gentle.

This inner strength has two sources. The deepest is the knowledge of one's relation to God. The other source of gentleness is self-control, and of course it is much easier when we are well-grounded in the sense of being accepted by God. When we seek our satisfaction on a deep level, the ups and downs of the surface don't bother us so much. A "gentleman" is one who is not overpowered by his own emotions — his anger or greed or lust or fear or grief. His self-containment is located at a deeper point that enables him to maintain a steadier state at the surface.

A third aspect to the ideal of the gentleman is the ability to put aside one's own comfort to care for those less fortunate or in greater need. This is the prime mark of "nobility." Again, this is a mark of strength. The gentleman is not a coward. He does not judge everything from the standpoint of fear: What will happen to *me?* What do I get out of this? I have to look out for myself. Even if he loses wealth, reputation, life itself, the gentleman intends to do what is right because it is right. When the value calls, the meek answer without hesitation. They alone are strong enough to do so.

These are reflections prompted by the English sense of "meek." What about the original Greek? The word is *praus,* and it names a virtue much prized in classical civilization. It relates to both athletics and politics, two Greek loves. It means basically control over one's passions, a kind of calmness. To be *praus* gives many advantages. Good judgment is the first. Not being carried away by one's emotions, one can estimate a situation more accurately and structure a fitting action. Every fighter knows that he mustn't lose his temper, because that loss will injure his intelligence for the task at hand. The same applies to other types of athletes. Neither anger nor fear can distract if one is to perform well. This is even more seriously the case for those who have responsible roles in affairs of state. If private emotions intrude, the wisdom of the statesman is lost.

A second advantage gained from being *praus* is that it gives flexibility. Uncontrolled emotion limits us to points of view and paths of action that seem to favor our particular short-term welfare. They deprive us of the wider and more objective vision that enables us to adjust quickly and appropriately to changing conditions instead of beating against a stone wall, insisting on what we want. Both the athlete and the politician have to be able to shift strategy expeditiously and effectively. This cannot be done if we are committed to our demand that we get our way.

Related to flexibility is resilience, survivability. It is a kind of elasticity that carries the ability to apply full energy to a new move, another perspective. If we are addicted to our own views and desires, we can't have this power, because we are tied, locked in, to our addiction. The energy isn't available. But if we are *praus,* we always have our energy "liquid," available with full cheerfulness, with no tightness or grudging. Consequently, we do not feel tired, drained, despondent, *de-spirited.* We are much more likely to stay fresh and good-humored. This is why Jesus calls to the weary and oppressed, saying he's got a cure for them, something that really helps.[2]

Now look at "lowly of heart." This is an interesting expression. It doesn't mean a lack of self-respect. Far from it. I think it can be usefully explained in terms of our physical sense of the center of gravity. Why do athletes bend their knees? Not to show submissiveness, but to obtain a stable base from which to act effectively. Lowliness of heart is a self-situating that is analogous to that. Take care to locate your heart in a sure foundation, broad-based, steady, solid. Avoid investing yearnings in something that's top-heavy, easily toppled, overthrown. Don't image yourself that way — don't think of yourself as better than others, or having power over a situation, or getting the upper hand even in small things. The trouble with that way isn't just that it's risky but that it's flimsy, not substantial, not sensible, not effective. Therefore take your stand on something fundamental enough to be productive and lasting. Invest your heart there, where it can "rest" — i.e., stand steadily without wobbling or losing its balance.

A deep foundation supports a larger structure. A sure foundation can sustain a wider area of action. If you act from a deep place and not "off the top of your head," you will make fewer mistakes and have more satisfaction and do a great deal more good in the world.

Being "meek and lowly in heart" is thus the way to find rest, both in the sense of relief from strains and tensions and in the sense of steadiness and a reliable base for action. This is intimately related to finding your real self and your real desires.

Exercises

Suggested reading: Psalm 37:3–8; Job 11:13–19.

All fasting is relaxing, letting go — and some of the energy bound up in self-defense then becomes available for joy in life and love for others. This "snowballs": more love and happiness means deeper prayer, which means more faith and more confident fasting, with more energy being released.

1. First be clear that you are not in this exercise to engage in blaming yourself or to deal with the judgment that you "ought not" to do such-and-such. That may very well be so, and some bad habits are indeed blameworthy, but that is in an ethical context, and we are now operating in a *therapeutic* context. We are trying to heal the situation, not judge, blame, or punish.

2. Introduce more quietness into your life. Turn off the TV, the radio, the stereo, other sources of stimulation. Slow down. Do fewer things; do them without rushing and savor them more. Avoid irritants. Take walks in silence, especially in beautiful natural places, if convenient. Sit in silence. Attend to the quiet, listen to it. Notice the not-doing. Enjoy it.

3. Practice relaxing the body, an excellent help to relieving the distress of negative emotions. Any time you think of it, relax by taking a deep breath and letting it all the way out in a sigh, saying softly or silently, "Let go!" or "No need!" (no need to be tight, to worry, to get excited, to be angry, to feel hurt, to insist) or "All right!" Remember that we will not miss our heart's desire.

4. Fast from angry or scornful words, from criticism or denigration. Remember to relax the body when these temptations arise. Speak softly, gently, kindly, especially to those at home. Others will catch your rhythm and be gentle and considerate

with you in turn. Fast from complaining and deliberately sub-
stitute words of approval, praise, and gratitude. This will force
you to look for the good aspects in everything, thus rearrang-
ing the emotional landscape, bringing the positive features into
prominence in the foreground and relegating the negative features to the vagueness of the background. Such emotional or
valuational arrangements are always of our own making. Now
we will experience more freedom and consciousness with respect to them and not be enslaved by them or believe that there
is only one way to regard our world.

5. When something has happened to upset you, especially if
you feel that your own behavior has been at least partly the
cause of whatever went wrong, take refuge in Jesus immediately.
Do not avoid him because you feel ashamed. This is precisely
the sort of situation that he is here for, to receive the wounded
at the field hospital. You will find ready comfort and support;
he will not make you feel worse, but better. So don't postpone
going to prayer.

6. Watch for a very small awareness gradually working its
way up through the layers of hurt and anger and whatever else
is impeding divine life in you when you start on this path. Watch
for a sense that somewhere underneath the various kinds and
levels of painful consciousness there is a sort of basic happiness.
The temptation is to deny this and to suppress it. We have made
a promise to ourselves that we will not be happy until our circumstances have changed, or we have been vindicated, or maybe
never. This is our way of getting even with life. But the foundational happiness is there, nevertheless, and it will continue
trying to rise to full acceptance. This is an important observation, closely related to the sense of the presence of God in the
center of our souls, the realization that at bottom we are all the
time "resting in the Lord."

Quiet Prayer: We have looked at prayer as a dialogue/
interaction with Jesus. The way I suggest now is just being quiet,
together with him, both of us appreciating a restful scene. The
idea is to let our inner rhythms come into resonance with his:

our irritation soothed by his calm, our lassitude energized by his confidence.

It is reported of Jesus that he would go out into the hills and spend the whole night "in the prayer of God" (Luke 6:12). This is how he got down to that foundation where meekness stands in balance, where he *knows* and is *sure* of his Father's love for him and his Father's powerful presence in him. Let us do an imaginative meditation with him.

The town is preparing for sleep. The day's work of preaching and healing and teaching is finished. In the last light Jesus slips away to the hills outside the village. He finds a flat spot with a bit of grass and a smooth rock behind for a backrest, where he can sit and see the stars. There is room enough for us and we sit nearby.

Now there is deep silence all around. He lets himself be quiet, just be there, look at the distant hills, the broad sky. We can feel the night wind rising. Wrap your cloak around and tuck it up to last the night. . . . We are in a good place. On the earth, under heaven. Inside God. Just be there. . . .

Feel the quietness in Jesus, the deep peace in him, the peace he gives us. Realize that it is rooted in his faith and knowledge of God, in his desiring only God's loving will. He doesn't bother making himself unhappy over the details of his life. He is full of confidence and strength. Let this faith, security, restfulness, peace, confidence, strength, seep into you. Catch his rhythm, resonate with his inner pulse.

A jumpy or distracted mind can be helped by being given a word or short clause to repeat. Try "One," "Rest," "Be still," "Peace," "Loose it and let it go," "Let go and let God," "My peace I give you." The Jesus-figure of our visualization may give us a word and say it with us. In repeating the word, we remain aware of the presence of Jesus and relate this word to our being with him. As we say the word on the out-breath, we can feel that we are letting go of tensions and demands, angers and hurts, hatreds, and rejections. As Jesus says the word with us, we can feel that he is sending his peace and his love for us into

us to crowd out or neutralize the negative emotions and attitudes. It isn't that we deny the anger or hurt, but that his grace
is stronger, more attractive to our attention, truer, more vital. It
fills our consciousness with healing and hope.

After a while we become aware that praying is going on. The
earth is praying, the rocks, the ground, the grass, the trees, the
distant rivers and the sea. The heavens are praying, the slender
moon and all the stars. The awareness of the reality, the presence and the dearness of God is becoming palpable. We are all
feeling it — the heavens, the earth, Jesus, ourselves. The prayer
of all the world lifts gently all around us, like a great heart beating, like a giant breath rising and falling in rhythm. The prayer
penetrates and permeates us. We rest in it and let it fill us. . . .

It is God's love. God's love in the earth, God's love in the
heavens, God's love in Jesus and in us. This is what we are, all
of us; we are made of God's love, breathing and beating, living
gently moment by moment.

We become keenly aware of being made by and out of this
pulsating divine presence. It surrounds and cradles us as a
Parent. We feel a profound reverence for it, a reverence that
reverberates through the whole creation and includes all these
presences of God — in the earth, the heavens, Jesus, ourselves.
And the more we feel this reverence, the deeper grows our sense
of reality, of sureness, security, and stability. We are resting on
the groundwork of reality in God's love.

Here is everything we desire. Here is where the heart finds
rest and has no inclination to move to this side or to that.

Jesus is very still. He has become part of this great prayer,
part of the wholeness of God's love, together with the earth and
the trees, the mountains and the stars. We are linked with him,
as the prayer passes through all of us: "Our Father, in heaven
and earth, may this name of yours always be reverenced!"

The wind stirs softly, caressing our faces, sharing its breath
with ours. God's breath, God's Holy Spirit, blowing through
us, all about us, inside us, outside us. . . . In and out, out and
in. . . . We in God, God in us.

— Four —

JOINING GOD'S UNIVERSAL, IMPARTIAL, CREATIVE LOVE

═══════════════ ❧ ═══════════════

WHAT IS LOVE? Surely it is one of those basic words, basic concepts, basic experiences that can't be defined. What would be *more* basic than love in terms of which you might explain what love is? Well, maybe "being." Maybe "goodness." So suppose we say that love is a will to being and to goodness. But it also has a feeling in it of self-gift, of extending ourselves out *toward and into* that which we love. We don't just will being and goodness from a distance. We in some way enter into that which we love.

This is the kind of love we mean when we speak of God's love. And, of course, God doesn't just *will* being and goodness; God actually *creates* being and goodness. Nor is that the end of the matter. It is not enough to say that God loves. We must also say that God *is* love. That isn't the case, according to Christian revelation. God is love. What does that mean? I think it means that loving isn't something that God can do or not do, or do sometimes or do toward some more and others less. God can't be God without loving. Take away the loving, or let it alter with circumstances, and you haven't got God. Loving, without any modification, without any condition, is the essence of what God is (1 John 4:8).

59

Mutual Unconditional Love

When Jesus was dealing with what we call "the Temptations in the Wilderness," trying out all the possible ways of ending the sentence that begins, "If you are the Son of God, then...," he thought about whether God's love for his people should be expressed in terms of bread and good luck and political sovereignty. What should it mean to be a child of God, to inherit divine life? And Jesus concluded that it had to be something much more profound than bread and good fortune and political or social standing. Those things are nice, but they don't reveal the riches of God. They are not entrances into the life of being-creating, goodness-communicating, self-sharing, unconditional love. Jesus held out for a deeper share of God's own life than mere good fortune in this world. Much as we would all like to have favorable circumstances in our lives, even the most favorable lot in this world will not satisfy our heart's deep desire, our capacity for the Infinite. If God *did* consent to manipulate our lives in such a way as to give us those temporal things that we think we want, God would be *underrating us,* selling us short, depriving us, tricking and betraying us, failing to acknowledge the capacity and the power that are really in us. God does not do that.

What God offers us instead is a love relationship that lives only in the love itself, not in any temporal manipulations, any finite gifts outside itself. It's as though God says to us, "I can't give you anything but love, my child. But that I give you in abundance. Is it not enough?"

I think it may help to appreciate what we've got if we realize that, historically, this is a new kind of religion. All the old religions were concerned with relating people to the whole fabric of nature, and within that context trying to control human fortunes, to gain life and prosperity, to avoid disaster. The oldest gods were nature powers who acted unpredictably; people tried to cajole them or placate them by offerings and sacrifices. The next idea in the ancient religions was the God who undertakes to care for and protect a certain people in return for their loyal worship and regular sacrifices. After an important period of maturation, this God was represented as desiring rather that the people practice justice and even mercy toward one another. A moral life was the sacrifice that God desired. If you offered such a sacrifice, God would bless you and see that you prospered.

This was a great improvement, we would say, but it's still a quid pro quo and it's still a concern with getting something done about the way we fare in the world.

We make deals with God. We'll be good, and God will see that nothing bad happens to us. But that isn't the way it turns out. And so we have a great problem when bad things happen to good people, especially *massively* bad things. We have the feeling that God isn't keeping his side of the bargain.

But even in the ancient world — and not only in Christianity — a new idea came into religious consciousness: the relation with God was not about controlling our fortunes in this world at all, as though God were a *means* to achieving *our* ends. No, it's just a love relation with God himself. The ups and downs of this life are not the main thing. The main thing is God; and we are invited to share in God's life by being loved by God and by loving God. And to keep the relationship pure, to make sure that it has to do only with love for love's sake and not with gaining anything for ourselves, God does not insult us by making any commitment with respect to controlling the kind of temporal life we're going to have. In the Song of Solomon God tells us, "Even if you offered all the wealth of your house for love, it would be utterly scorned" (8:7). This is why the great lovers abandon everything, leave everything behind. It is only by not presuming to offer their beloved anything less than themselves, and themselves alone, that they can demonstrate the depth of their love. They say only, "I am my beloved's and my beloved is mine" (Song 6:3).

Now I admit that this is strong medicine and not a little scary and hard to hear and accept. But if we have faith and patience, support one another and really *think* about it, we will see that this is the only way we can be satisfied, the only way to find God surely and to fulfill our heart's desire. We are created, said St. Augustine, "turned toward God," and our hearts will remain restless until they rest in the Infinite Being. We are made craving the God who is unconditional love, and until we experience that love unconditionally, we will know — on some level of our being — that we haven't yet got to the heart of things, to the foundations, to the uttermost limits.

Therefore, we have to recognize that what will really satisfy us, enable us to fulfill ourselves, to be what we are meant to be, to be *all* that we can be, is participating in unconditional love; and that means that it has to be unconditional on both sides. God loves us without conditions, and we love God without conditions.

The Rich Young Man

Now I want to propose a meditation and another depth in fasting. The meditation will be drawn from the story of the Rich Young Man who asked Jesus what he must do to inherit eternal life and who was eventually invited to sell all he possessed and join Jesus. Notice the theme of renouncing and embracing again. Our fasting, which I want to talk about first, has to do with the renunciation of possessions.

Some possessions are those things that we rely on to make us feel good, secure, and important. Some of them are external things, material goods, social activities, personal relationships, honors and positions. Some of them are internal things, compensatory fantasies, defensive attitudes, even sacred hatreds, which are our private ways of striving to cope with an experience of life that hurts, that makes us feel frightened and unfulfilled and unfairly dealt with. We also have our favorite demands on life and our deeply lodged resentments and complaints to present to God. And we have our accepted despairs, our lost hopes, and we defend and protect them, too. We have the rejections that we have experienced in life and that we have either agreed to internalize, to believe about ourselves, or sworn to avenge — or maybe both.

Jesus is saying to us that it's very natural and understandable that we would hoard such possessions, life being as hard and bitter for most people as it is, that on their own level such possessions are often justifiable, valid. But he is revealing that there is a deeper level. He sees our "possessions" as our being "possessed." We suffer from our possessions because they don't solve our basic problem; they don't help us find our heart's desire but rather distract us from it. On the level of the possessions, we think that what we want is a God who will give us victory against our enemies, heal our illnesses, and fill us with the good things of this human life. But this doesn't usually happen, and there is a very good reason why it doesn't happen: we are being helped — in this terrible way — to go to that deeper level.

This, then, is the fast that I propose. Let us give up believing that God puts *any* conditions on his love for us. Let us give up thinking of ourselves as unworthy and take Jesus' word for it that worthiness has nothing to do with it; it doesn't come into the picture at all. God sends sun and rain upon all indiscriminately and radiates all with his self-giving love. So let us fast from being anxious or shy in our relationship with God. There is nothing to worry about. Thoroughly believe that God loves you just as God loves Jesus. That's the Gospel; that's the Good News.

So let us believe it and also give up putting any condition on our love for God. Let us not expect — or even be interested in — rewards or favors for our good deeds. Let God's love be the greatest thing in our lives. Let us try to be willing to let go of all those "possessions" by which we are "possessed" and prefer God himself to any benefit we could possibly desire as finite creatures.

When we do this, we realize that we're not left in the state of being merely needy, finite creatures. When we accept God's unconditional love and when we love God unconditionally, we enter into the divine life itself. The life of God is shared with us because that's what the life of God *is*. It is a self-sharing, unconditional love among the three divine Persons, and they share it with us. All we have to do to be in it is start doing it: accept the love that is offered unconditionally and return it unconditionally.

Now let us do the meditation. The version of the story that I give here is pieced together from both Mark and Matthew in order to cover all the points I want to address.

As Jesus was setting out on his journey, a man ran up to him and asked him, "Teacher, what must I do to inherit eternal life?" And Jesus said to him, "You know the commandments: 'Do not kill, Do not commit adultery, Do not steal, Do not bear false witness, Do not defraud, Honor your father and mother.'" And the man said to Jesus, "Teacher, all these I have observed from my youth." Then Jesus, looking upon him, loved him, and said to him, "You lack one thing. If you would be perfect, go, sell what you have, and give to the poor, and you will have treasure in heaven; and come, follow me" (Mark 10:17–21; Matt. 19:21).

I stop the story at this point because we are going to put ourselves in this young man's place, and we may give a different response from the one he gave. Let us pursue the meditation in this way: You are a person who is very earnest about your religious life. You have been questing and searching, studying, praying, going to church, trying to be good, doing everything you can to live near God. Your heart is still craving more; you are still unsatisfied. Although you have traveled a good deal on the spiritual path, you have now come to the place where you feel that there is something more, maybe something surprisingly different from what you have been working on, that is, keeping the Commandments. What is this something more?

You have heard of Jesus, that he is a teacher with power, with a new and liberating message. He does not speak as the scribes do. He speaks from the heart, from his own experience, as one having authority, one who knows. Perhaps he knows what this "something more" is, this something of which you are in search. And so you come to him. Your question is burning. "Teacher," you ask him, "what must I do to inherit eternal life? . . ." And Jesus recites the Commandments for you. "But, Teacher," you protest, "I've *been* doing that. For a long time already. It doesn't seem to be enough. Surely there's something more?" And then Jesus looks at you and loves you.

Everything is in this loving look. You understand that Jesus isn't loving you because you've kept the Commandments. It would be closer to say that he loves you because you yearn for something more. But really this love doesn't have any "because." This loving look is Jesus himself, radiating, reaching out to you in joy that you are right on the verge of making the Great Discovery, the discovery that everything is given up for the divine life, everything is renounced for love. "Yes," he says to you, "you are right. There is something more. One thing is still lacking to you. If you really want to be perfectly satisfied, if you want to have your heart's desire, then let go of everything else and just be with me."

You understand that his love itself is part of the invitation, part of the "wakening" work of Jesus, his way of loosening us from our attachments and "possessions," our demands and disappointments, and drawing us into the life that alone will make us whole, holy, and happy. You had thought that Jesus would know the secret. You had hoped — but scarcely dared to believe — that he would tell you. And he has not only told you; he has opened the way for you actually to attain your heart's desire.

He has told you in two ways. One is with words, a sacramental way, a baptismal way: renounce and embrace. Renounce everything else, and embrace my life. Give up all that baggage inside. None of that is meaningful where we are going. I provide whatever is needed when you travel with me. To embrace me is to let slip, to forget, all your former insistences on having your life run a certain way. We will be journeying together. I do not promise you a comfortable trip, but I will always be with you. We will share the same life.

The other way Jesus tells you the secret is just in this looking at you and loving you. Because that's *it* already. That's what the Life is, that's what you'll get if you renounce all the rest. Jesus looks at me and loves me. The whole revelation is in that, if we can penetrate it, if we can receive it.

"To all who receive him . . . he gives the power to become children of God: who are born, not of good fortune or of any of the finite circumstances of this world, but sheerly of the love of God." Therefore, "gird up your minds, wake up and think about this seriously, and set your hope fully upon the grace that is coming to you in the revelation of Jesus Christ. . . . For it is written: 'You shall be holy for I AM HOLY' " (1 Pet. 1:13–16). "His divine power has granted to us all things that pertain to life and godliness, through the knowledge of him who called us to his own glory and excellence, by which he has granted to us his precious and very great promises, that through these you may . . . become partakers of the divine nature" (2 Pet. 1:3–4).

We must realize that this is the Good News tradition handed down to us. St. Athanasius in the third century wrote: "We are made consorts of the divine nature by the communication of the Holy Spirit." St. Cyril of Alexandria, in the fifth century, added, "The Holy Spirit acts in us, sanctifying us and uniting us to himself and making us participants in the divine nature." And he repeated, "We are made consorts of the divine nature and are said to be 'born of God,' and so we are called 'gods,' not merely elevated to supernal glory by grace but actually having God indwelling and abiding in us." And St. Augustine reaffirmed, "God said, 'Men are gods, deified by grace.' "

This is the secret that Jesus knows and that he confides to us in his love for us; for he says, "All that I have heard from my Father I have made known to you" (John 15:15). He heard the gist of it in that voice from heaven at his own baptism: "You are my beloved child. In you I am well pleased." Jesus is telling us that the same thing is true of us. In his loving look, Jesus is showing us his inner sense of himself, in which we learn of *our* own deeper self. He is saying to us, "Come, follow me, join my life, listen with me to the voice that I hear, for my Father also says to you: 'You are my beloved child. In you I am well pleased.' "

All this he gives us in his loving look. When we are profoundly convinced that he has revealed the truth about us, that we are indeed well-loved children of God, partakers of the divine nature, we will be free, we will be liberated, redeemed. And the divine life, which is naturally and spontaneously self-communicating, will flow out from us also, just as it does from Jesus. Having freely received, we will be able freely to give. We will be able to give our best to our family, to our work, to our community and society, to our play and recreations, to whatever we do in the love that is the life of God.

Sharing Divine Life

What we want, we said, is to share in divine life. But divine life is unconditional creative loving — giving being and goodness to others. We know that we have entered into this divine life when we start loving freely and unconditionally, when we start seeing everyone else as kin to us. As 1 John 3:14 says, "We know that we have departed from the place of death and entered into the place of life because we love all our kindred."

That's what Baptism is all about — and the Lenten preparation for the renewal of our Baptism at Easter. It's about crossing from death to life. We depart from — renounce — trying to gather the means of life to ourselves, to hoard them, to keep them for ourselves rather than sharing them with others, because such a selfish way only leads to death. It's like breathing: we speak of the "breath of life." As long as we're breathing, we're living; breath is life. So let's hoard our life, let's hold our breath. But holding our breath isn't living; it would kill us, if we could do it. Breathing is going in and coming out; living is sharing. Hoarding any of the goods of life — material, social, intellectual, emotional — goes against our own deepest nature and deprives us of the springs of being at our root, which is the divine creative act, the existence we derive from our divine Progenitor, the God whom Jesus calls "our Father." This is why Jesus reveals to us the basic truth that "if you seek to save your life — 'save' in the sense of sequester, hoard, hold back — you will lose it," because that will prevent you from living. Whereas, "if you are willing to let your life flow from you freely, for the sake of the Good News that God's love and life are constantly flowing into you — and through you — then you will live without limit."

If we see what he's getting at, then we become willing to let go of building ourselves around efforts to preserve and enhance our finite lives in this world and by a kind of relaxation and release give ourselves to expending our lives in the light of the Good News that we are all children of God. This is what unleashes, sets free, redeems, the unlimited life of God in us. It is this truth that frees us, as Jesus promised it would, if we can ever really know it. Once we're free, we begin to function as what we truly are, creative lovers who can will being and goodness to all, even as God does.

This is why I say that Jesus reveals this truth to us instead of saying that it is a commandment or some requirement that God makes before giving us a prize. It's not the case that this is a kind of choice in which we can obey God and gain the reward or else disobey God and take the punishment. That's not really a very good image, model, or metaphor for our situation. It's something much more intimate than that. Jesus is *confiding* to us the principle of divine life. This is, we might dare to say, the rule by which the Persons of the Trinity live, thoroughly giving Themselves to one another. It is being shared with us, not demanded of us.

It is important, therefore, it seems to me, that we let Jesus share his life as he wishes and not put obstacles in his way, by denying that it's possible or by trying to water down the immensity of what he's doing, or by continuing to say the kind of thing that Peter said, "Depart from me, O Lord, for I am a sinful man." We empathize with Peter; we know what that feels like, where he's coming from when he feels impelled to express himself that way.

But now we must consider Jesus' point of view. He wants Peter to come to this point because this is a crucial moment in the crossing over from death to life. But if Peter gets stuck there, in that position, in that view, in that set of feelings, and just keeps repeating that he is unworthy, then Peter is actually resisting what Jesus is trying to do, which is to enable Peter to break out of that prison. So when Jesus comes to us with his recognition that we too are children of God and calls to us to give up our former notions of what was important in life and join him on his road and share his life, becoming everything that he is, let's not beg off by pretending to be modest or humble or unworthy or incapable. When he says he wants to make saints of us, don't tell him he can't do it!

The fasting that is appropriate to this set of ideas is therefore simply this: Let us give up believing that we can't live this divine life. Let us stop saying that that's for somebody else. "Of course Jesus could live like that, but he's the Son of God. You can't expect the same thing of me." If we persist in that kind of attitude, what does that do to his efforts to awaken us, to release us, to share his life with us? He *does* expect the same thing of us. Otherwise, what's the point of making disciples? He keeps affirming that we *can* do the works that he does (and greater), that it is our *birthright* to do such, that we are brothers and sisters of his and share his life in every way. Remember that his own point is not to do wonders to amaze or to prove anything, but rather to release the captives, to preach the Good News, to spread unconditional love abroad, to live in the light of God's love. Since he has said we can live this divine life, let us fast from saying to ourselves and one another, explicitly or implicitly, that we *can't*.

We must also resist the temptation to say that we must wait

until after we are dead or until the end of the world to share in this divine life. We may call to mind what Jesus said to Martha after Lazarus was entombed: "Your brother will rise again." "I know," answered Martha, "at the end of the world, on the last day." That is, sometime in the far future, the indefinite, unknown future, when the world is unimaginably different. Jesus sweeps all that sort of imagery away and obliges her to confront the reality of life *now.* "I AM the Resurrection and the Life," he declares. "Do you believe this?" Crossing from death to life takes place whenever you consent to believe it, to acknowledge that you *can* enter into and share this divine life that Jesus opens to us.

So, how do we do it? We do it by entering into the heart of Jesus. In him we do our believing, in him we do our praying. This is the equivalent, I think, of what St. Paul said to the Romans: "*Put on* the Lord Jesus Christ" (13:14). And Paul also says that this is not to be postponed: "It is *now* the hour for you to be awakened." To the Philippians he says, "Think the same way as Christ Jesus," and he spells that out a little: "If there is any encouragement or support to be found in Jesus—if he acts as an advocate, stands by you and takes your part, offers consolation, soothing, cheering, and bracing words, shows you love and exhorts you, welcomes you to participation with him and common life in his Spirit, if he gives you affection and sympathy—if you find this in Jesus, if he has that kind of mentality, then complete my joy by being of that same mind yourselves, having that same love for one another. Look not only to your own interests but also to the interests of others" (Phil. 2:1–5).

We are to enter into the mind of Jesus so that we think his thoughts; we are to enter into the heart of Jesus so that we love with his love. Notice that this is not quite the same as "imitating" Christ. Imitating implies looking at a model and then copying it in some medium external to it. We are concerned rather with a real *sharing* in the Spirit, in the life of God, a sharing that is interior to us and interior to God. It isn't as though we look at the works of Christ and then try to make a copy or parallel in our own lives. Rather, we are caught up into the flux of the divine life itself, and from our position there — in Christ, as a current in that ever-moving life in which we ourselves live and move and have all our being — from *there* we participate in doing what that mighty life is doing.

Up to this point we have been concerned with finding our own individual, personal fulfillment, our own heart's desire. It turned out that that desire was to share in divine life, and this we are enabled to do through the liberating love of Jesus. He loves us, and this liberates us from the necessity of self-defense and awakens us to our own capacity for happiness and love-sharing. We begin by loving him in return, and that means becoming very close to him. And this is the turning point in our spiritual life, turning from a preoccupation with our own personal fulfillment to the fulfillment of others, of all, of God. That God's will may be done on earth begins to become a real prayer, a real desire. And not only for *our* sakes, but for *God's* sake. For as we are more and more drawn into the divine life, we find ourselves more and more looking at things from a *sharing* point of view. We are decentered from ourselves and then gradually decentered from all of the groups to which we conceive ourselves as belonging and from whose viewpoint we tend to see the world. Ultimately, I believe, we will be able to decenter even from the exclusively *human* viewpoint and appreciate how we share our lives also with all other living creatures and the rest of the marvelous cosmos. For, as St. Paul prophetically said, the whole creation is eagerly waiting for the revelation that itself is made up of "the children of God."

The Healing of the Leper

We begin to make this turn in our point of view by entering into the heart of Jesus, by joining his point of view. This is part of our love for him and his love for us. It is his way of sharing his life with us. We join him in what he sees, what he feels, what he does.

Now I want to try to show you how we can have some first-hand experience of this. The story for meditation is taken from Matthew 8, the Healing of the Leper.

When Jesus came down from the mountain, great crowds followed him, and a leper came to him and knelt before him saying, "Lord, if you only will it, you can make me clean." And Jesus stretched out his hand and touched the leper, saying, "I do will it; be clean." And immediately his leprosy was cleansed.

You begin the meditation by imagining that you are the leper. You say, "Lord, you have only to will it, and you can make me clean.... You have only to will it." And Jesus stretches out his hand. You see him reaching out to you. He touches you, you feel it, you feel the warm, firm, loving, confident touch of his hand. And you hear him say, "I do will it. Be clean. Be well. Be whole. I do will it."

He is pouring his entire attention into you, loving you with all his heart, all his mind, all his soul, and all his strength. "I do will it," he is saying with his whole being. "Be healed. Live, and be happy." Feel the strong current of that will flowing into you. "I do will it. I do will it."

Now, as you listen to him say that, over and over, gradually let yourself pass over from being the leper to being inside Jesus. Say with him, "I do will it. Be well. Be whole. Live. Be happy." Feel the power of this will in him. You are united with him now, flowing together with him like a river of love. Looking out through his eyes, you see the leper before you, a human being in disease and distress and loneliness. You reach out to this person. You touch the leper. You are full of love for this person. You are completely focused in your will that this person be healed. All your heart is concentrated on this, all your mind, all your soul, all your strength. You are flowing together with the heart of Jesus as he gives the fullness of his love; you are flowing together with the mind of Jesus as he gives all his attention; you are flowing together with the soul of Jesus as he foresees health and happiness in this person. You are flowing together with Jesus' strength; you sense the power, the energy, in him and it energizes you to love and will with him. "I do will it," you say with Jesus, looking with him, touching with him, willing with him.

And you feel the power of the divine will as it moves through Jesus and through you united with Jesus, a tremendous will to goodness of being, flowing through you, catching your own will into its mighty current, flowing out and into the person of the leper. "I do will it. We will it. Be whole. Be happy." And you see the leper relax and change. The stress and fear and pain and sadness disappear. The signs of the disease fade and are replaced by the glow of health. You feel that your life has gone out from you and into this other, who now lives in wholeness, and you rejoice. You realize that God's will, Jesus' will and his love, your will and your life, and the leper's will and life are all flowing together in love, in wholeness and happiness. You are all one flowing life.

You have given yourself — together with Jesus — to live in this other person, and you have seen that other person filled with life and the ability to give life and love in turn. You have joined Jesus in pouring himself out to the leper. As Jesus has been willing to live in this other person and to welcome this other person into his life, so you go with him, with Jesus, out to the leper and receive the leper also into your heart. All three of you are now living together, sharing one life of love, which you feel as a dynamic current of willing being and goodness to one another, a flowing current of living love. And, having given your life in this way, you feel how your life has *increased*, that you are more fully and deeply alive than you were, that you are living a bigger life. You realize now how true it is that the more you give your life away, the more you are really alive.

Furthermore, this will to wholeness, which Jesus has, is extended to all, without any discrimination, any distinction, any partiality, any preference, or any condition. It has to be that way, or it's not the divine life. When we enter into the divine life, as we do through Baptism, that's what *we* do, too. "Be complete," Jesus tells us in the Sermon on the Mount, "as your heavenly Father is complete — whole, inclusive, not leaving anybody or anything out." Jesus had read in Deuteronomy (10:17) that God is "not partial and takes no bribe." And he had seen the significance of the sun rising on the evil and on the good, and the rain falling on the just and on the unjust. And he had known by the love in his own heart that the only way to manifest God in the world is by loving all, without any difference, without any condition. This is the life we are called to join.

This goes against our worldly wisdom and ways. We keep wanting to reward some more than others, to honor some more than others. But that's not how it is in the kingdom of heaven. Every worker in the vineyard gets paid the same, regardless of how long each worked. All are rewarded equally; all are honored equally. In fact — as we eventually find out when we get deeper into the spiritual life — notions of "reward" and "honor" themselves disappear. As St. Paul so well said, only love remains. But it remains for all, overflowing, not measured, infinite in all directions.

Exercises

This kind of meditation, if you keep practicing it, will give you a sense of what it is like to be inside Jesus, to see and feel and will with him. And you will find that you *can* do it. Practice by taking other instances from the Gospel stories in which Jesus has expressed his love and join him in perceiving, feeling, willing, acting. Then take instances from *your* life, in which you want to learn to love as Jesus does. It may be someone you want to help or someone you find difficult. Let Jesus focus his will to well-being on that person first, and then you join in, letting your heart and mind and soul and strength be caught up into the outflowing energy from Jesus. Then let yourself flow with him. It's a little like standing next to someone who can sing the alto or bass line. If you stand close and listen, you can sing along with that person. In this way you will gradually be able to join Jesus in loving even your worst enemy.

Perhaps he has told us something of how he goes about it in the "searching" and "seeking" passages: "Seek and you will find," search for the hundredth sheep until it is found, for the lost coin until it is found. What would happen if we sought for the child of God in everyone we know until we found it? Jesus can do it, and he promises that if you enter into him and abide there, you can do it too.

Start with people you naturally care for. Advance to people about whom your feelings are neutral. If you are still able to do the meditation fully, gradually try people you have uncomfortable feelings about, starting with the least difficult and giving yourself plenty of time. Take care, too, not to pray that they be "healed" of whatever you dislike about them. Rather, let Jesus look at the person in his usual way of searching and penetrating until he finds the level on which that person is his kin, another child of his Father. Join him in that seeing. Then feel what he feels when he finds another relative, feel the life-sharing that he feels. Let his power carry you; don't force yourself. Just bless these persons in their own (deep) terms, whatever those are — a kind of blank-check blessing, directed to their secret heart and true desires, which we believe to be ultimately directed toward God.

Remember that our fasting at this point is founded on our realization that there are no limitations on this love, no discriminations, no distinctions of rank or position, no more or less. It is universal and completely impartial. This is probably the most revolutionary thing that Jesus taught, that God's love is perfectly universal and impartial and that we, if we are to realize our divine heritage, will love the same way. Read Matthew 6:43–48 and 20:1–16. Can we give up ranking people, categorizing people, preferring some classes to others? Can we give up any sense of privilege or of being especially favored? Can we give up identifying ourselves as a member of a class that is discriminated against—even if it's true? Can we rethink the deference behaviors that we practice or that we expect? Can we express courtesy and respect without implying that one is superior to another? Think about this, imagine ways of doing it, practice them.

Finally let our "prayer" begin to become something that we carry with us at all times, not just something that we "do" at a specified time. Let our "abiding" in Jesus, in his universal love, full of vitality, become our prayer. Read John 15:4–5, 7–11. As we practice this, we will gradually realize how creative the divine love is. Not only does it make all things to be, but it is constantly energizing new forms, and especially it is dwelling in us as *our* creativity, our share in the divine creativity. It makes us to be and be like itself, to be an extension of itself, for God dwells in us, living, loving, creating through us.

— Five —

THE BODY OF CHRIST

===================== ࢟ =====================

THE TRANSFORMATION that we are seeking and that is conveyed in the Easter mystery concerns not only ourselves as individuals but ourselves as members of the community. The community, likened to a living body, has some principle of organization and operation by which it lives. The message and example of Jesus say that the principle of organization and operation that the community has been using has to die and a new one has to replace it so that life rises up anew. He points out the principle we have been using, he rejects and destroys that principle, and he institutes a new principle. This has been his teaching and his work all along, and it is especially and dramatically encapsulated in the events of Holy Thursday.

On Holy Thursday, sometimes called Maundy Thursday from the Mandatum, or New Commandment, given on that occasion, there are two great sacramental, or mystery, events: the Washing of the Feet and the Holy Communion. These two actions show us two different views of social organization and behavior and summarize what we may call the "Before" and "After" pictures of ourselves that Jesus offers us.

First, the Footwashing. In that place and at that time, people got their feet dirty walking from one place to another. A mark of hospitality when you arrived as a guest was the host's seeing that you got your feet nicely washed. He provided a servant to do this. Probably his wife did it for him if he didn't have servants. Footwashing was a way of indicating who was who on

77

the social ladder. Servants washed the feet of their lords and
masters. Lords and masters didn't wash the servants. Women
waited on men; men didn't wait on women. That's the way society was structured. We still do it that way, don't we? How are
things done at the office? Don't the people in inferior positions
have to make themselves agreeable to those in superior positions and perform little menial services for them? How about
the way names are used on the job? If you are an inferior,
don't you call your boss Mr. So-and-So, while he calls you
"Joe" or "Jenny"? He's familiar with you, as if with a child,
while you have to be formal with him, as if with a parent or
adult. It's a way of reminding you of your subservient position. If you have a maid to clean your house and cook for you,
don't you call her "Mary" while expecting her to address you
as Mrs. Smith? That keeps the roles straight. She's the servant;
you're the mistress.

It's not only the lords and mistresses that like to keep the
roles straight. Often enough the servants want the traditional
order preserved, too. Just look what happened on Holy Thursday evening. In the place of a servant to wash their feet, Jesus
takes off his coat, rolls up his sleeves, gets a towel and a basin of
water, and sets about washing their feet himself. This horrifies
his disciples. He is their lord and master. He's out of character,
out of his proper role, when he undertakes to wash their feet.
Peter — not for the first time — feels it necessary to correct him:
"Lord!" he exclaims, reminding Jesus of his title and position
and expected behavior. "Lord! You shall never wash my feet!"
Don't you realize what you're doing? he might as well be saying. You'll upset the whole social order by this kind of behavior.
We can't have this. If you start acting like a servant, what are
the rest of us supposed to do? If I let you wash me, why I might
even be expected to wash my wife's feet! People won't know
their place anymore, what their station in life is.

But Jesus just rocks back on his heels, fixes Peter with an im-
placable eye, and says, "Unless I wash you, you can have no
portion with me." Either you consent to this, or you can't par-

ticipate in what I'm doing. Put like that, Peter has to accept it or get out, so he consents. But it's very disturbing, all the same. Very disturbing. After he has washed everybody, Jesus puts his coat back on and sits down again. "Now," he says, "do you know what I have done?" And here I will embroider a little what he says. "We have grown up in a society organized on the lord/servant model. You and I have been playing that game. In that game I am the lord and master. But I have given you an example of my conception of my real relation to you. Don't think that this is some sort of extraordinary condescension on my part. This is typical of what I have been doing for you right along. I didn't come here to be served but to serve, even to give my life as a ransom for the captives of ignorance and sin. I'm setting an example. If I have washed your feet, you also ought to wash one another's feet.

"In other words, this whole structure, in which some people are lords and other people are servants, has to be washed away. The kingdom of heaven is not built that way. Look at the Romans. You see that they have some people in superior positions who dominate those under them, and their important people expect to be treated with deference (Luke 22:24). You, who intend to be my disciples, are not to be like that. You are to be neither lords nor servants. Didn't I tell you from the beginning that my Father is impartial, sending rain and sun on the righteous and the unrighteous alike? Love and respect all. Consider no one either inferior to you or superior to you. No one is more worthy in God's eyes than another. Remember the story of the vineyard? The workers went in at different hours of the day, so they worked different lengths of time. But when the owner paid them at the end of the day, they all received the same wage. Naturally the people who had worked hard all day in the heat thought that they 'deserved' more, that a difference should be made between them and those who had worked less, and that they should be shown some preference. But they got what they had agreed to, what was fair. There was no preference, no contrast. No one was slighted or deprived, but no one was set above his fellows either. There are no 'unworthy' people in God's eyes, nor any who are 'more worthy.'

"This is different from the way of the world. The workers who wanted more, who felt that a distinction should be shown between themselves and the latecomers, were feeling and speaking on the basis of the way of this world. Their complaint was not just that they didn't get more money — for they were paid in full according to their contract. But what angered them was that 'you have put these others on a *level with* us.' They felt that *leveling destroyed the value*. The value came from the distinction. Do you see how that is playing 'lords and servants' with values in general? That is the point.

"This has been the structure of this world. All our relations to one another have been conceived in these terms. We have built up a temple of ideas and behaviors on this cornerstone. What I have done in washing your feet is *destroy that temple!* I have renounced and demolished the whole lord/servant pattern. I will no longer call you servants but friends. This is the new temple I will build, the temple of my own Body (John 2:21), of which you all shall be members" (cf. Eph. 2:20–22).

When you get to know Jesus from the inside, you know that he does such things, that he intends to renew things *totally,* that he's very radical, going to the *root.* He doesn't just change the answers; he changes the questions. And he doesn't just change the questions; he changes the assumptions on which the questions are based. For instance, that trick question he was asked about the seven brothers and the one wife: in the resurrection, whose wife would she be? He doesn't give an answer that accepts and respects the question. He doesn't say, "Well, she'll now revert to the first husband," or, "In heaven you can share spouses." He dismisses the whole foundation of the question: There isn't any marriage at all.

Or consider the question of which of us shall have the greatest honor and the most privileged position in the new kingdom. There isn't going to be any such thing as "greatest" or privilege or even position. That's the sort of thing he does. He requires you to shift your way of thinking about things on a very fundamental level. You do not merely move the furniture across the room; you may have to forget the furniture altogether because he's going to tear the house down! Radical. Revolutionary. "Behold, I make all things new!" Not the same old things, repaired and freshened up, but things you never thought of, things "it has not entered into the heart of man to conceive." And he is by no means finished yet. We are in the midst of this transformation.

The Holy Community

Now Jesus begins to present the second picture, the "After" picture, the picture of the transformed society and the transformed individuals who compose it. He takes the bread laid for supper, whose sharing had always been a sign of unity, blesses it, breaks it, and gives it to his friends, saying, "Take this and eat it. It is my Body which is given for you." He also takes a cup of wine, blesses it, and gives it to them, saying, "This is my Blood of the New Covenant, which is poured out for you and for many" (Mark 14:24). And then he adds, "Do this, as my memorial."

This is the central Christian rite and sacramental celebration. It is a tremendously rich symbol; it has a great deal to say. I will let it offer a "Communion Paradigm" to replace the "Domination Paradigm" of footwashing. Two realities are intertwined here, the Body of Christ as the personal presence of Jesus (who is the Word of God) and the Body of Christ as the church, the holy community composed of ourselves. One of the wonders of this great sacrament is how the latter is created from the former.

The Body of Christ is a good metaphor for the holy community, because it is personal and intimate. Sharing your body with someone symbolizes sharing your life, your inmost selfhood. The fundamental meaning of the Eucharist is life-sharing.

When Jesus gives the bread, which he calls his Body, to his friends, he tells them to "eat it." What happens when we eat anything? It sustains our life; it gives us energy; it repairs our being; it enables us to grow. This is surely the intention of Jesus in thus feeding us. He means to give himself to us to vitalize us: to energize us, to restore us, to enable us to grow. That is the most obvious thing. But notice something more: what we eat had been something exterior to us, something "other than" ourselves; but once we eat it, it becomes ourselves. That which we eat is no longer external to us, no longer something "other than" ourselves. This is profoundly revealing of the love of Jesus for us, the degree of life-sharing that he intends. He wants to mingle his life thoroughly with ours — and of course, ours thoroughly with his. He says this explicitly in the speech he makes after the Supper, in which he says, "I am in you and you are in me." And he likens that commingling to his life-sharing with the Father: "as the Father is in me and I am in the Father."

But when this has happened to each of us, when each of us is engaged in life-sharing with Jesus, then he is living in the whole community of us: his Body has been intimately joined to the body of every person in the community. And since his Body is the most vital and the most vitalizing — the most life-giving — element in any of us, all of us together constitute a kind of extension of his Body. And that enlarged Body acts as any living body does: it grows and unifies and develops; it supports diversity within itself by being secure in its unity; it operates as a system, without superiors or inferiors.

Jesus says it is like a vine composed of many branches. Notice that he does not call himself the "trunk" and us the "twigs." He is the *whole* vine, and the vine *is* its branches, the branches *make up* the vine. And his Blood — the wine — flows through the entire system as a unifying stream, a single life principle.

This systemic structure is emphasized by Jesus' words, "Do this, as my memorial." Let us relate these words to other times when he said, "Do this." For instance, consider the closing words of the Sermon on the Mount, which remind us that it is all very well to know something or even to understand something, but we will be blessed only if we do what we know or understand. Jesus sets the example, which he expects us to copy:

"Follow me," he says. He himself does what he sees the Father doing, and he earnestly recommends that we do what we see him doing. It is not enough to admire Jesus doing something and praise him for it. He isn't looking to be acclaimed "Lord, Lord!" He wants us to do the Father's will, just as he does. All these works that he does, he insists, we can do also, and even greater works. So when he says, "Do this" of something, he doesn't mean make a ceremony out of it and play-act *him* doing it. He means that we should do the same thing ourselves.

In this case, the case of Holy Communion, the case of feeding others with one's own body, one's own life, when he asks us to "do this" as his memorial, I suggest that he means that if we would all feed one another as he has fed us, then he would have a fitting memorial of his work among us. He even says this plainly: "Love one another as I have loved you." This cannot be done by stopping short of giving ourselves as food, as nourishment, as life support and life enhancement, to one another. "Greater love has no one than this, that one lay down one's life for one's friends." *Friends,* he says. No more talk about lords and servants. This is a completely different structure of human relations. "There is neither Jew nor Greek, there is neither slave nor free, there is neither male nor female; for you are all one in Christ Jesus" (Gal. 3:28). This is the new temple, the temple of his Body, a new structure in which human life is enshrined. Each of us is now another Christ, feeding all the others with our own body and blood. Remember that our own lives have first been thoroughly mingled with the life of Jesus, who first fed us with his Body and Blood, so that his life took up residence, so to speak, in us; it took over our lives, in fact. "I live, yet it is no longer 'I,' but Christ lives in me," St. Paul says. So when we share our lives with one another, we are sharing Christ with Christ. And yet we are also truly sharing our own selves.

A Living Memorial

What makes the difference between the old temple and the new is that the structural principle of the old temple is value rooted in scarcity, based on goods that cannot be shared. If we identify ourselves and our worth in terms of what we have or are that contrasts with what other people have or are, if we value ourselves in terms of goods that are *not* shared, then we feel alienated and separated and insecure.

The structural principle of Jesus' new temple is that it is built on values that *can* be shared, that *must* be shared, in fact, in order to be the values that they are. Speech, and the ideas conveyed by it, art and beauty, good will, friendship, joy in fellowship, all these values, which are peculiarly human values, are essentially shared values. You can't have them by yourself; and the more you share any of them with other persons, the more you have of them yourself. Jesus is the very embodiment of the value that must be shared, the divine love. In the old temple we try to hoard bread for ourselves, food that cannot be shared because whatever another has I then lack, and whatever I cling to, I cannot simultaneously give. But in the new temple the bread *multiplies* by being shared, feeding thousands, and Jesus himself is the bread that is shared. When we share this bread, our life enlarges, our sense of Body expands, we feel integrated and secure. This is the living bread that comes from heaven, from the domain of divinity, and those who eat of it do not die but have unlimited life.

Now notice a very important point. Because Jesus is a bread that must be shared, he cannot do the eucharistic action alone. If he did, it wouldn't be perfect sharing. If he's to share his life, then he has to share also the capacity for sharing itself. This is where Holy Communion as a very private, personal, intimate bond between each individual and Jesus expands and overflows into the community. The key is that the more each of us is united to him, the more each of us has to join him in doing what he does. That's what being united *means*.

Jesus says to his friends, "Do this, as my memorial." It is as if he had said, "I want you do the same thing that I just did: give your lives into your friends and kindred, all the other children of Our Father, even as I have done: feed them with your own bodies, share the last drop of your blood with them, live in them and let them live in you. Form one great living Body among you all. That is the memorial I want, a living memorial, built out of all my friends, my sisters and brothers, one Body, sharing one life. And I myself will be present in it too. It will be my Body. I am not leaving you orphaned. Wherever even two or three of you gather together to share your lives in my name, I am there, I am present. Really present. I recognize the union of all of you, all of us together, as my Body. And you are to know it also as your Body."

Exercises

1. Go back in this chapter to the part about "lords and servants" (see p. 77 above). Search your life for instances of playing the domination/submission game and consider whether you can give that up. The "fasting" of Lent is becoming still deeper and more serious.

See how many instances of this relationship you can identify. Begin with the family. Then count relationships that are not necessarily institutionalized this way — such as individual encounters — but in which the unspoken issue is to determine who's going to be dominant. Think also of history. Think of nations. Think of economic institutions. Think of religious institutions. Think about whether this practice of domination is consistent with the teaching of Jesus. Consider whether the submissive partner bears some responsibility for the situation too and maybe should get some assertiveness training, organize with like-minded people, become more politically active, or take whatever might be the appropriate action.

Now get a little more subtle. Consider *why* we are involved in these dominant/submissive patterns, besides their being a hold-over from primate social relations, evidently selected-for because they gave some advantage to group survival. We, as human beings, are now reaching for another stage of growth, beyond the natural animal world. The Christian life is sometimes called a "supernatural" life; in that metaphor, Christ is the "first mutant," who passes his "genes" or form of life to those who come after him. But what psychologically is supporting the old, natural, primate form of life?

We believe that we are separate, limited, vulnerable beings who need all the protection we can get. A good defense is a strong offense. If you don't get ahead, you're falling behind. You can't tell how good you are except by comparing yourself with someone not so good — or beautiful or rich or smart or powerful. Do you recognize these principles? They're the ones we're used to using. Work with these ideas. See if you can see how they lie at the foundation of our urgent need either to dominate or to be dominated — and thus get off the hook of having to make decisions and take responsibility, and thus also perhaps be supported and taken care of as well. And when you see clearly that they lie at the foundation of our lord/servant ideas, feelings and behaviors, then see if you can see that they indeed *lie* at that foundation: see that they are *falsehoods,* from the point of view of the child of God.

This is where the flip happens, where the revolution occurs, where you pass from natural to supernatural. When you become a child of God, those principles, those assumptions, no longer apply to you. They're not true for you anymore. And if you have always been a child of God — but just didn't know it — then they were never true for you, and you were basing your life on falsehood when you believed in them. This is why, in the baptismal promises, you are asked to renounce Satan, the Father of Lies (John 8:44). It is this old way of thinking, feeling, and acting that has to die in order that the new way of living, as a child of God, can rise up.

2. Now consider how different the resurrection life is, the life

of Holy Communion. See that the very basic view of who and what we are is different. It's not a question of your behavior merely, of being "good" instead of "wicked." You can't change your behavior unless you change your feelings, because your feelings will always get the better of you. And you can't change your feelings until you change your ideas, your viewpoint, the way you see the world. We are asked to "love our neighbor as our self." We can't do that, because we see our neighbor as being precisely *not* our self, as being someone quite other than ourselves, as being even a potential threat to our self. In fact, we will say, it's the neighbor's being other than our self that enables us to have a self at all. We exist only by the contrast, by not-being the other. I am I by not being you. We identify ourselves by mutual negation. That's what gives rise to lord/servant relationships, and that's what has to change, die, and be replaced in order for us to enter into the resurrection life, eternal life, and be able to love our neighbor as our self.

This change appears in the Holy Communion. Instead of mutual negation, we see mutual affirmation. Each person is feeding each other person with their own life: the most radical and complete affirmation you can give. But it isn't destructive of the giver. The bush burns but isn't consumed. It can go on burning and giving forever, because that is its true nature: it is a Giver. And so the more it gives and shares and affirms, the more it is what it is, the more it realizes and fulfills itself. The Giver says, I am I by giving myself to you; I live in you and you live in me. Jesus tells us that this is the life of the Holy Trinity and that we are to live like that: we are to be one in the same way that the three divine Persons are one.

This is a completely different perception of reality. And that is the level on which the revolution has to take place, the level of perception. Until you see the world differently, you can't feel differently, and until you feel differently, you can't act differently. See how the perception differs: instead of seeing others as not-self, we see them as also-self; we are members of one another. "Self" isn't a matter of *dividing* the world into parts; it's a matter of seeing and loving the whole. Jesus refuses to be a "divider" (Luke 12:13: the true "family inheritance" is the divine life, something that can't be "divided"). What clothes the Christ is a seamless garment. There isn't a place where I leave off and you begin; we are profoundly involved with one another, even as the Father is in the Son and the Son is in the Father. You don't need to ask to see the Father, as if the Father were somewhere else and Someone Else rather than the Son; if you see the Son, you see the Father; Father and Son are one. And we are to be like that, says Jesus.

3. Can we give up, fast from, limiting our sense of the Body of Christ and the Holy Communion to the ceremonial sacrament of church ritual? Can we see that the supernatural grace revealed by this visible sign is more, ever more, still expanding? Can we understand that this spreading and deepening in meaning is the way the mysteries are intended to act in us?

If we come to see that the church ritual is a sacrament (external sign) of the living community, what shall we say about refusing to celebrate this sign with people who don't belong to our particular church? Does Jesus ever turn someone away from his table? And for that matter, does he decline to be "really" present unless the ceremony is conducted by a person with the proper credentials? Perhaps he is as present as he chooses, when and where and how he chooses, and none of our legalisms can keep him out! Or perhaps, if we turn our sisters and brothers away, he goes away with them. Are we ready to fast from the assumptions and beliefs that have made it possible for us to consent to some of these exclusionary practices?

4. As we fast and pray in this way, we become able to love our neighbors as ourselves and to act accordingly. So in your meditation on Holy Communion consider how this revolutionary view of our reality and our relations to one another could change how you live in your daily life and also how it could change the way the whole world is organized. Can this vision of truth be a pinch of yeast that will eventually "leaven the whole lump"? If we have faith in this vision, will it grow from being as

tiny as a mustard seed to being a great tree? Will this secret that we hear, as it were, whispered into the ear, become so prevalent in our society that it is being shouted from the housetops?

I can imagine that I join friends in celebrating Jesus' Holy Communion of the "cells" of his Body by giving a bite of food to my neighbor and whispering, "This is my life given to you." In my vision I then turn back and find that another neighbor is handing food to me with the same intention, saying, "Here I am; let me nourish you." I look around the table; everywhere I see all of us feeding one another with words of love. (Look at the picture on the cover of this book.) And I realize that this is indeed the Christ, the Child of God, who has come and is coming into this world. This is the Christ that must grow and spread and replenish the earth. We are all to be members of this one life, to fill out and complete the Body of Christ. We are the new temple of the living God, whose life is manifested in our mortal bodies as our inner nature is being renewed day by day (2 Cor. 6:16; 4:10, 16). What its limits are, no one knows.

5. Perhaps the real presence of God has no limits (Ps. 139:7–10). St. Paul tells us that "all things" were created in Christ and through him and for him. So is he not present to them all? And if we dwell in him, then we have a presence to them all also. We have no call to feel alien in this universe; it is no stranger to us but, through Christ, our extended "body." The entire cosmos is the created image of the Holy Trinity, the origin of all "good gifts," all eucharist: it is built up as diversity within unity, bound together by exchanging the various sorts of energies appropriate to each level of its organization, culminating in ourselves, who are able to love one another as persons. Perhaps this is the ultimate Body of Christ.

Can we experience ourselves in these terms? Can we feel this sharing, exchanging of energies, being food for one another, finding our good in the good of the whole living Body? The more we enter into the mind and heart of Jesus, the more we will be able to share his vision of reality, his love for all. Let our prayer be seeing/feeling/intending from the point of view of

Jesus as he gives himself as food to his friends, thus to dwell in
them, thus to constitute them an extensions of his own Body. Let
us try to take our place in the Body, "doing this" as he asked,
in our turn.

Let our prayer now really take place "in Jesus' name," and
let us consider that that name is "Life-Sharing." Let us pray always now from inside this living Body, in chorus with all the
rest of the Body in its unique polyphonic music. Pray through
everyone and everything. Let all of them pray through you. Feel
the beat of the common Blood, breathe with the common breath
as the Holy Spirit prays in the Body (Rom. 8:26–27; Jude 1:20;
Eph. 6:18).

— *Six* —

THE SPIRITUAL JOURNEY AS
THE WAY OF THE CROSS

═══════════════════ ঞ ═══════════════════

W E HAVE SEEN the beginning and the end: how we start off in a world in which we operate in terms of domination and submission and how Jesus holds before us the vision of a world of Holy Communion in which we all feed one another in love. But how exactly do we pass from one world to the other? We have to die — that is the answer that is given all over the world; not only Christianity knows that, all religions say the same. That is to say, your false sense of yourself has to die — and you will be surprised to find out how subtle that can get. But that is the way, and in Christianity it is represented as the mysteries — the sacred events — we call the Stations of the Cross, or the Way of the Cross.

It is a spiritual journey, its various incidents representing experiences that we have in our own journey into the necessary death whose other side is eternal life. In Jerusalem people walk through the streets that Jesus (perhaps) actually walked through on his way to Calvary, and in many churches there are pictures or bas reliefs illustrating the traditional events of that last journey. But these are mysteries, that is, they are external signs of interior graces, participations in the divine life, so we must seek their interior meaning. St. Paul urges us to "put on" Christ, and he describes his own life as being Christ living in him. We are to walk in the footsteps of Christ, not so much looking at him as ourselves *being* in his position. It is from this point of view that we will study the Way of the Cross as a mythic exposition of the spiritual journey; the outward signs will be interpreted as inward realities, our own interior experiences.

This chapter will not have separate exercises at the end, for the whole text here will serve as exercises. We will meditate on the first nine stations in this chapter, and the following chapter will develop themes appropriate to the remaining stations. I would add only that in order to go on this journey, we must dedicate our travel to the salvation of the world, as Jesus did, not merely to our own liberation. Each of us, as we move from station to station, contributes to the true-being, the free-being, and the well-being of the Whole.

The First Station: Jesus Is Condemned to Death

This is our condition, our situation. When we become interested in spirituality at all, when we find out what is involved, this is where we begin. We know we have to die. There are two levels to this realization. In the first place, we realize with some vividness the contingent and temporal nature of our earthly life, short at best and always uncertain. We all are supposed to know that we are going to die, but most of us don't really realize it. A certain king once asked a wise man what was the most astonishing thing he had found, and the wise man answered that everyone, though observing that all living things perish, believes "I will not die." Part of this is just not giving attention to and accepting a fact. But it is also an intuition of our vocation to eternal life, the intimation that we will *not* die. But even if "we will not all die," nevertheless, "we will all be changed." This change is coming upon us, whether we will or no. We are condemned to die. That is the first level.

The second level has to do with our voluntary assumption of the spiritual journey. The first thing that happens to us when we decide that we are going to open ourselves to transformation is that it is revealed to us that we must die in a spiritual sense. Something even more intimate to us than our natural bodies must die. Our sense of self must die. Jesus spells it out plainly: if you seek to save your life you will lose it; only if you lose it in the Gospel will you save it.

When we first set foot on the spiritual path, we believe that the self that has to die is the selfish self, or the ego as grasping and stingy, cruel and calloused, thoughtless and lazy. We want our false self to die, the self that is crabby and self-centered, vain and ambitious, that suffers from various faults and weaknesses. We agree: this self is to be condemned to death.

The Second Station: Jesus Receives the Cross

We accept the burden of spiritual practices. We undertake to go to church, to read the Bible, to say our prayers, to participate in charitable works, to try to overcome our faults, to be kind and patient, and so on. We may even undertake some meditation practice or become heavily involved in social service work. Perhaps we decide to change some important habit in our life that we feel is not in line with God's will for us. This is the program that is supposed to help us pass from our old life to the new, and we accept it.

We may even be enthusiastic about accepting the cross. We've started a whole new life. Look at the saints; we're going to be like them. It just takes a little devotion, a little work. But we're happy to do it. It's new, it's romantic. We may become very pious, very devout. We may spend much of our time doing our spiritual exercises. We may build our whole life around them. We may try to persuade other people to come do it the way we do; this is the only way! We're excited about the whole project.

But Jesus remarked that someone planning to build a tower had better figure out how much it is going to cost and see whether he has the means to finish it. Or if he is challenged to go to war with a big army, he'd better calculate whether he stands any chance of winning with the forces he has. This is going to be a protracted struggle; don't think it isn't.

The Third Station: Jesus Falls the First Time

We very soon find out that it's not all smooth sailing. We're not able to live up to the high ideals we've set for ourselves. We keep doing things unworthy of our high calling. This hurts and puzzles us. We don't do the things that we want to do, and the things that we don't want to do, those are the very things that we find ourselves doing — in spite of all our good resolutions and all our efforts! The temptation was too much for us, or it happened before we could catch ourselves, or it was just too much of an effort to give that extra bit. This is disconcerting and fills us with chagrin. We may even be tempted to throw over the whole enterprise rather than be humiliated by these failures.

Jesus told a parable about different kinds of soil onto which seed was thrown. Some seeds fell along the path and were eaten by birds. This is the fate of those who don't understand the Gospel message at all and fail to give themselves to the spiritual journey. Some seeds fell on rocky ground, sprouted a little, but having insufficient root, soon perished. These are those who receive the Gospel with great joy at first but cannot persevere because they have not put down a deep enough root; their interest and their excitement are superficial. Their religion is a fad and an entertainment. As soon as the excitement fades, as soon as it's no longer an interesting social occasion or a stimulating intellectual exploration or an emotional experience of a new and moving color, they drop it for something else. Some other seeds fell among thorns, and while they struggled to prevail, the thorns eventually choked them and they died. These are those who try to live the Gospel but are constantly pulled the other way by the ways of this world. They may believe they have obligations that force them to do things that they know are contrary to their ideal. Or they may be so caught up in ambition that they can't stop, can't get free — they think — from the complications in which they have involved their lives. Or they may have become addicted to pleasures or practices or relationships that are harmful and yet be unwilling to forsake these. Like St. Augustine, they may *want* to be free, but they keep postponing their release. All these types make excuses for themselves and endeavor to justify their behavior.

Mere busyness and being burdened with duties are not the same kind of impediment as such distractions — in fact, they are not necessarily an impediment at all. Many good people feel that they "don't have time for a spiritual life." But spiritual life is not another activity for which you have to take out extra time. It has to do with the disposition in which you do whatever you already are committed to doing — as well as, of course, the choice of which things you do. Even the busy person, the parent, the worker, the person who gives extra time to charitable causes, can readily be one in whom the seed grows up to fruit.

The fruitful ones are the fourth class, the case of the seeds that fall on good soil and are able to come to maturity without impairment. Remember that in this story we represent the soil, not the seeds. We don't have to have a certain kind of seed in order to grow up in the Gospel. We only have to have faith and good will. The Gospel was originally preached to the poor, the ignorant, the oppressed classes of society, the criminals, the outcasts, all the marginal people. And they were the ones who embraced it and passed it on to us.

If we are "good soil," then when we fall — in spite of all our good resolutions and our outward piety and our strong devotion — we will pick ourselves up and go on, understanding that this is going to be a long journey and no one has indicated that it will be easy. What did we expect?

But this is a point where we may be tempted to give up. If we are rocky soil, we may just shrug, tell ourselves in some disguising language that it's not fun any longer, and go in search of something new. If we are thorny soil, we may choose to pretend that we are still faithful, but we just can't do it *this* time — very

like someone who is supposed to be on a diet or giving up smoking but keeps making excuses for not adhering to the projected
reformation at *this* moment. This moment has to be an excep-
tion, but we still want to be accepted as being "on" the diet or
the renewal program. We may take the position that our falls
"don't count." These are the temptations and the alternatives
that we face at this stage in our journey.

The Fourth Station: Jesus Meets His Mother

For those of you who are interested in history, we have to say
that much of this story is legend. That Jesus carried the cross,
at least part way, and that he spoke to the women of Jerusalem is recorded in the Bible, but some of these other stations
have no historical support. However, as markers of psychological stations in our spiritual journey, they have value. So when
we regard the whole Way of the Cross as we have it from tradition as a mystery, as an outward representation of interior grace,
we can still take the legendary portions seriously and look for
the graces they have to convey.

When we have realized that falling is part of the journey
and when we have confronted the temptations and understood
something of their different natures, we may turn back to our
beginning. We may look for the ground of our spiritual life. We
may seek the matrix in which this whole life of ours first began to grow. The figure of Mary represents the mother of our
spiritual life. The shock of the falls and the temptations, the
realization of the difficulties, has sent us back to search for our
origins. What kind of being are we? How did we get started on
this quest? What has been feeding us until we could take charge
of our own lives? That is, what has been "mothering" us?

There are various ways that we can work with these symbols — as there are with all symbols. I will propose one, but you
may find others. I begin with the definition of sacrament, the
outward sign of interior grace, and I say that the Blessed Mother

means some graciousness of God *in me.* I remember Thomas Merton saying, "Mary is the Mother of Christ in us." A very helpful clue. I find that what has been mothering me is some aspect of my being, largely unconscious, now becoming conscious as I meet it face to face at this point in my spiritual journey. Something in me was overshadowed by the Holy Spirit at the very beginning and has been trying to grow in grace ever since. I didn't know it was there. The Christ in me, the graciousness of God in me, is conceived by the Virgin Mary in me — something very deep and unknown but prepared by God as the way in which this divine life should come to birth. This aspect of me is a virgin. What does that mean? It means unity, integrity, not being adulterated or mingled with another, not being torn, being continuous or uninterrupted, being single not double. There is a ground of such being in me, somewhere. It is from that ground that this yearning for God and freedom and all the values of the spiritual life has grown. It protected these aspirations when they were only embryos, nurtured them, enabled them to develop.

At the very moment when I have to confront my faults and failings and realize that it will be no easy task to overcome them or lose them, I am comforted by the revelation that there is also in me some deep source of life and protection. I draw strength from this and new heart to go on. This insight tells me that my struggle is worthwhile, that in spite of appearances it is blessed. Whenever I feel down, I can turn back to this Blessed Mother in me for comfort and renewal of my faith. Hidden away at the foundation of my being, she is always singing, "My soul magnifies the Lord and my spirit rejoices in God....He has done great things for me."

This is an important moment in the journey of transformation, the transformation from the worldview of footwashing to the worldview of holy communion, and the shift in the sense of selfhood that alone can bring that about. The discovery of the Holy Mother at the foundation of our self means that our self is not exactly as we had thought it was. We had thought our self was completely caught up in the various worldly interests that superficially characterize it, looking out for its advantage and comparing itself with others. But now we see that there is more to it than that. There is also a level on which we don't do that sort of thing, a level that is not involved in these separating and falsifying and sin-engendering beliefs and feelings, a level that is full of grace. It is that level that continues to nourish us, even while we continue to struggle with our faults and failures. But the old sense of self has been breached; some opening has been made to something that lives by a quite different principle than does our superficial sinful self.

The Fifth Station: Simon of Cyrene Helps Carry the Cross

I have described the station as Simon helping to carry the cross, slightly at variance with the Bible account that says that the cross was laid on Simon or he was compelled to carry it, because helping is a better metaphor for our journey story. No one is going to take the whole cross off our shoulders and carry it for us. But we do receive a great deal of help, especially if we can recognize it and accept it.

Once we have broken through to the realization that there is something in us that supports and mothers our journey of transformation, once we have discovered that there is more to what we call our "self" than we had known, we are open to discovering that there are many helpers about. This again takes place on more than one level of interpretation. The first is the ordinary sense of other human beings in their roles as helpers to us. At this stage in our spiritual journey we become more sensitive to the positive influences coming to us from other people and more grateful. Many things that we had taken for granted we now become acutely aware of as gifts of love to us. Gratitude begins to become a more prominent emotion in our lives. We think of our parents and other relatives, of our ancestors, even of the long line of those who went before us in this life and all that those people did and suffered to make our lives possible. In the Easter Vigil we will sing the Litany of the Saints, a kind of roll call of our ancestors in the faith and a memorial to those from whom we have received so much. They represent people from all times and places whose lives have been contributions to the lives of others. We are members, one of another.

This works both ways. St. Paul urges us to "bear one another's burdens and so fulfil the law of Christ." He says this in the context of someone's being "overtaken in any trespass." Those on firmer ground are to "restore" the fallen one "in a spirit of gentleness" and watch themselves lest they too be tempted. Now that we understand ourselves somewhat better, now that we see how easily we succumb to weaknesses in spite of our enthusiasm for the spiritual life, we can have compassion on others similarly constituted. Other people, inside, are not too different in these respects from the way we are ourselves. We begin to feel for them sympathetically. Furthermore, since we discovered that there is also a deep mothering principle of grace and goodness in us, we know that there must be such in everyone else, no matter how depraved they may appear to be. Jesus warned us not to "judge by appearances, but give a true judgment." Therefore we begin to be able to believe that God loves everyone as a dear child and extends grace to all. This enables us to have a kind of supernatural respect for every person and to know that we stand in the midst of a great mystery and cannot write people off as unworthy or rejected.

Gratitude and sympathy combine to motivate us to be helpful in our turn. More sensitive now to how the little things affect us, we are mindful of the little things we do or omit to do. Not all our consciousness is tied up in just paying attention to ourselves, how we feel, and whether things are going well for us. Our sense of self is stretching, its boundaries becoming permeable, translucent. We are expanding to include many more people and even other creatures and to include not only those contemporaneous with us but those who have gone before and those who will come after. Our concern for the future becomes a sincere and real concern, and we appreciate what is called "ecology" — all creatures living together and relating to one another — in a new, intimate, immediate, and spiritual way.

Another line of interpretation directs us to look for helpers within ourselves. Simon of Cyrene was a stranger. He just happened to be on the street at that time and was grabbed by the Roman soldiers and pressed into carrying the cross. He had no intention of getting mixed up in this business. But it changed his life, for the Bible records the names of his children; evidently the whole family became Christians. Now there may well be elements of ourselves — memories, feelings, abilities — that we never thought to involve in what we call our "spiritual life," but which might make major contributions to it. There is some reason to think that for every problem we have, we unconsciously possess the power to deal with it. The discovery of the mothering principle in ourselves helps us to believe and understand this. We are usually too prone to believe in our weakness, our inability to cope or change. We often want to find support for our claim that we "can't" and resent being encouraged to hold that we can. At this station of our spiritual journey we become more open to the belief that there *are* unknown, not yet discovered or involved "helpers" in the depths of our lives and consciousness, and we become more willing to search for them and bring them into participation in our transformation process.

A good way to develop these powers is to pray for them. Father Max Oliva, S.J., has outlined a prayer he calls the "Freedom Prayer."[1] He applies it when he finds a particular need in himself. For instance, he noticed that he had a tendency to be jealous and to want to be loved in a way that was special by people to whom he and others were ministering. With full faith in the grace of God, he prayed for "freedom from the need to be special." Every time he caught himself feeling jealous, he would repeat the prayer, just once, and then rest in the confidence that God's grace, working at some deep level in himself, would come help. And it did. He gradually got completely free of that need and the feeling of jealousy. Notice that the ability to *observe* the failing, the ability to *want* to be free of it, the *faith* that God's grace would free him, the ability to *resolve* to pray for that grace, the ability to *persevere* in repeating the prayer until the freedom was complete — all these "helpers" were present in himself. Observing abilities, wanting abilities, resolving abilities may have been developed by us in other contexts but can now be brought into the transformation process as vehicles of divine grace. We all have companies of such helpers in ourselves; we only have to commandeer them and involve them explicitly in our spiritual journey.

"Helpers" sometimes come in strange guises. "Helpers" in this context means events or circumstances. A lot of things happen to us in our lives that we — in our ordinary or merely natural consciousness — consider not helpful at all but rather harmful. If we want to get the full grace from this mystery we need to look at this. Probably all of us know of people who have suffered a major reverse in their lives but who claim in retrospect that this was the best thing that had ever happened to them. They found the event a "helper." Those are hero stories, and we recount them as miracles. But then in our own daily lives we continue sorting what happens to us into two piles, helpful and harmful. St. Paul (Rom. 8:26–28) tells us that *everything* works together to good for those who love God. He says this in the context of how the Holy Spirit "helps us in our weakness": "the one searching the hearts knows what is the mind of the spirit, because according to the will of God he supplicates on behalf of the saints." This is a curious sentence and it is not perfectly clear whether the one searching the hearts is the Holy Spirit or whether "the mind of the spirit" refers to the Holy Spirit. But it does suggest that there is something going on deep in our hearts, some searching, that is connected with knowing the mind of the spirit — some hidden truth, perhaps about ourselves — and that is further connected with supplication on our behalf. We are "the saints" referred to; there is no question about that. All this is the action of the Holy Spirit in us, and the result of it is that all things, not just naturally favorable things, but *all* things, "work together, synergize!" for our good. The strange things that happen to us, which seem so unfavorable to us, these very things can be dealt with by the Spirit that moves on a profound level in us, searching our hearts and knowing what really goes on in us. When we open ourselves to this Spirit, we can realize how all these things are being "worked together" to our good in our spiritual journey. Strangers who become helpers come into our lives every day in the guise of everything that occurs.

The Sixth Station: Jesus Leaves His Image with Veronica

This is a totally legendary event. The story says that a woman from the crowd on the street took pity on Jesus as he passed on his way to Calvary; she came forward and wiped his face with her kerchief. Afterward it was found that the imprint of his face was left on the cloth. The woman's name was Veronica.

This is a good example of how a sacred story that is admittedly fiction can nevertheless be a medium of grace, because what it *means* is true. "Veronica" is a word made from the Latin *vera,* meaning "true," and the Greek *eikon,* meaning "image or likeness." There may have been a cloth with the imprint of a face on it that was believed to be a miraculous image of Christ. As distinguished from painted pictures of Jesus, this imprint was said to be the *true* image, taken directly from his face itself. In any case, the Veronica story dates from quite early times and has been part of the tradition for a long while, indicating that people relate to it meaningfully.

One meaning that could be drawn from the Veronica station by a twentieth-century person is a reflection on the compassion we show when we accept another's effort to help us. In the midst of his pain Jesus was able to recognize and accept the unknown woman's desire to express her concern for him. What she did didn't stop the pain, but it was a gesture of love and he was open to receive it from her. Even when he had every natural reason to be completely absorbed in his own distress, he could open up to someone else, even a total stranger. He could begin a new love relationship when he was on the verge of death.

Applying this to ourselves, we see that the ability to receive is as important as the ability to give. Giving can make us feel powerful and superior to those to whom we give. Being able to receive neutralizes this feeling, brings us into better balance, and helps us to transcend both feelings of power and feelings of weakness. The self begins to realize that it does not have to be characterized by either.

This is close to what the station has to teach, which is the meaning of the "true image." Now Jesus himself is the "true image." The Epistle to the Colossians says plainly, "He is the image [eikon] of the invisible God." And the Gospel of John declares, "No one has ever seen God; the only Son, who is in the bosom of the Father, he has made him known" (1:18). And the image is true, very faithful. Jesus can answer Philip, who has asked to be shown the Father, by saying, "Whoever sees me sees the Father."

But we also are images. Immediately after calling Jesus "the image of the invisible God," the Letter to the Colossians calls him "the first-born of all creation." And Romans says that we are to be "conformed to the image of his Son, in order that he might be the first-born among many brethren" (8:29). John promises that "to all who received him...he gave the power to become children of God," being born, "not of blood nor of the will of the flesh nor of the will of man, but of God" (1:12–13). This is clearly a reference to our supernatural life and as such is to be taken most seriously, I would even say literally.

There is a very interesting passage in the Gospel according to John that can be studied in this connection. It not only reinforces the note of the heritage of divinity but it points to the manifestation by which the true image can be known. The event recounted takes place in the temple in Jerusalem, where Jesus is teaching in the portico of Solomon. He has made the claim "I and the Father are one," and some of his hearers, shocked by what they understood as blasphemy, took up stones to stone him.

> Jesus answered them, "I have shown you many good works from the Father; for which of these do you stone me?" [They] answered him, "We stone you for no good work but for blasphemy; because you, being a man, make yourself God." Jesus answered them, "Is it not written in your law, 'I said, you are gods'? If he called them gods to whom the word of God came (and Scripture cannot be broken), do you say of him whom the Father conse-crated and sent into the world, 'You are blaspheming,' because I said, I am the Son of God? If I am not doing the works of my Father, then do not believe me; but if I do them, believe...that you may know and understand that the Father is in me and I am in the Father." (John 10:30–39)

The Scripture passage referred to is Psalm 82:6: "I say, 'You are gods, sons of the Most High, all of you.'" Christian reve-lation evidently both takes this with the greatest seriousness and stresses the pragmatic test for it. The First Letter from John says, "See what love the Father has given us, that we should be called children of God; and so we are.... Beloved, we are God's chil-dren." And here comes the test: "No one born of God commits sin; for *God's nature abides in him,* and he cannot sin because he is born of God. By this it may be seen who are the children of God" (3:1–2, 9–10). And listen to how this is supported by the Second Letter of Peter:

> His divine power has granted to us all things that pertain to life and godliness, through the knowledge of him who called us to his own glory and excellence, by which he has granted to us his precious and very great promises, that through these you may escape from the corruption that is

in the world because of passion, and become *partakers of the divine nature.* (1:3–4)

But here again is the pragmatic test for the true image: "For this very reason, make every effort to supplement your faith with virtue, and virtue with knowledge, and knowledge with self-control, and self-control with steadfastness, and steadfastness with godliness, and godliness with brotherly affection [*philadelphia*], and brotherly affection with love [*agapē*]." If these things abound in us, says Peter, then we will be fruitful in the "full knowledge" — *epignosis* — of Christ.

Now we are right at the heart of the Christian mystery and revelation, and this station of the True Image represents the stage in our spiritual journey at which we begin to perceive these deeper meanings and to learn something about our real selfhood. Not only are we to abandon identifying ourselves as lords or servants, powerful givers or weak receivers, not only do we have a totally pure mothering principle hidden somewhere in the depths of our being, but we are called to become partakers of the divine nature and to be fruitful in the full knowledge of Christ. This is tremendously releasing. If we have glory from God, what need do we have to seek glories from one another by our crude and petty competitions? What do we need to defend, to protect, to strive to enhance? The foundation of the old sense of self as defined by its various characteristics and relations in this world has been dissolved from under us. We begin to understand ourselves in a way quite different.

The Seventh Station: Jesus Falls a Second Time

At this stage in our spiritual journey we have become rather different people than we were when we first set out. Well, of course, that is to be expected. If we weren't, it wouldn't be a journey. If we have gotten this far, we must have persevered, and that in itself is quite an accomplishment. We must have coped somehow with the constant little daily failings without giving up and without giving in, either. And probably we don't have the big faults we used to have. We have conquered many of our tastes and tendencies and temperamental indulgences that we saw to be contrary to the life of charity that we are trying to lead. We not only *don't do* most of the "bad" things we used to do, but we *do* a number of new "good" deeds. Our life is to a noticeable extent purified and expanded.

At this point we run into a completely new set of faults. They arise out of our virtues. The least subtle of these are the desires for acknowledgment: we want gratitude for our good deeds, recognition for our conquest of our bad habits, admiration for our devotion, or respect for our understanding of the spiritual life. A more subtle set consists of ideas and feelings that we are now different from the common run of people, "worldly" people. We protest that this is simply so; why not admit it? But it's *separating!* We are the ones who understand that separation is the thing to avoid; *they* are ignorant or consumed by ill will. But in thinking this way, we are guilty of the very separation we are committed to avoid! And a still more subtle sin is the complacency and pride we feel on the one hand and the shame and anger we feel on the other hand when we become aware of our pride and wish we didn't have it. We can even be ashamed of our shame, because we understand how it is just an inverted form of pride.

All of these thoughts and feelings show how attached we are still to our sense of self. It is still enhancement of ourselves that we are trying to achieve. Only now we perceive that it is "spiritual" enhancement that is the valuable state. So we try to attain that. But the value still comes by contrast and by recognition: we have to be different and better and "set apart"; we have to be the "elect," the "chosen" ones. We may even have some special name for those we are set apart from: the heathen, pagans, gentiles, unbelievers, materialists, the ignorant, or however we choose to characterize "them." The contrast helps us to see that we have attained the value. When other people look up to us or commend us for our virtue, then we feel good about ourselves. Or even when we look at ourselves and compare ourselves with worldly types. The "good feeling" is a feeling that the self is safe; it has got some treasure to sustain itself; it has succeeded in preserving and advancing its life, though on the much more subtle level of "spirituality."

Jesus was very familiar with this trick of our consciousness. "Beware of practicing your piety before men in order to be seen by them," he warned, "for then you will have no reward from your Father who is in heaven." Not that God will refuse to bless you, but that your action will in itself block the blessing from infusing your life. The desire for admiration is a life principle so contrary to the divine that the two can't coexist. You can't serve God and Mammon; you can't live by the God principle of agape and at the same time want praise for yourself. So when you give alms, says Jesus, don't sound a trumpet to call attention to the fact. Try to hide it even from yourself, so you won't reflect on your good deeds and say to yourself, "What a good person I am!" Don't let anyone know if you are fasting; don't make a show of saying your prayers. You may get recognition and human praise, but that will be it: that's your "reward."

Jesus told a story about distinguishing yourself from what you take to be irreligious people. It's the famous story of the Pharisee and the publican. The Pharisee thanked God that he was "not as other men." He did a lot of religious exercises. The poor publican, of course, was outside the Law altogether, collaborating with the enemy, collecting taxes for the Romans. Jesus himself never drew a line between himself and sinners. He went to dinner with publicans; he talked with harlots. We have no reason to think that he "preached at" them, either, or otherwise "talked down" to them. He must have united himself to them in some very convincing way, because they apparently took to him very strongly. The idea is that there must be no separations. Jesus is not a divider.

Another interesting story is the one about the sons of Zebedee — sons of thunder, Jesus laughingly called them! — who came in one day, all hot and bothered because there was another man, over the hill, who was preaching and doing miracles in the name of Jesus, and, they complained, "He doesn't walk with us." He doesn't belong to our church. "Shall we call down fire and brimstone on him?" Jesus refuses to see the separation: "If he's doing good deeds in my name, he won't soon be saying anything against me!"

It is also in this context that we can appreciate the rationale behind the admonition "Love your enemies." The whole idea is to remove separations, to realize unity. That's the life principle of the divine life; if you want to share in the divine life, that's how you do it: outgoing love, concern for the other, union with the other, complete forgetfulness of yourself. It is not remembering yourself and then neglecting — or worse, "sacrificing" — yourself, but rather not remembering to reflect on yourself at all. You won't get caught in the trap of being ashamed of your spiritual pride if you'll just keep looking ahead: put your hand to the plow and don't look back to see how well you've done; just keep on plowing straight ahead.

Notice that the cure for these new and more subtle errors is not meditating on them and being sorry for them. That only focuses more attention on ourselves and our desire for spiritual perfection. What we have to do is turn away from thinking about ourselves at all and keep putting our attention on others. We have to resist the temptation to check up on ourselves, measure ourselves, see how we're getting on. Where examining our conscience used to be a beneficial exercise, it is now harmful and has to be abandoned. Just keep your eye on Jesus, keep following him; don't look back, don't look down.

Remember what happened to Peter when he walked on the water. As long as he kept his whole consciousness focused on Jesus and the call, "Come!" he was doing fine. But then he began to reflect on what he was doing and right away he started to sink. Jesus called this loss of focus "doubt." It means "doubling" your mind: part of it thinking about what you are doing, and part of it thinking about the fact that it is *you* doing it and how well you are doing it and what praise you're going to get (or anyway, deserve) for doing it. Keep your eye *single,* says Jesus. That's the only way to be fully enlightened.

The Eighth Station: Jesus Speaks to the Women of Jerusalem

This story is taken from the Gospel according to Luke:

> There followed [Jesus] a great multitude of people, and of women who bewailed and lamented him. But Jesus turning to them said, "Daughters of Jerusalem, do not weep for me, but weep for yourselves and for your children. For behold, the days are coming when they will say, 'Blessed are the barren, and the wombs that never bore, and the breasts that never gave suck!' Then they will begin to say to the mountains, 'Fall on us'; and to the hills, 'Cover us.' For if they do this when the wood is green, what will happen when it is dry?" (23:27–31)

Jesus himself had mourned over Jerusalem: "O Jerusalem, Jerusalem, killing the prophets and stoning those who are sent to you! How often would I have gathered your children together as a hen gathers her brood under her wings, and you would not! Behold, your house is forsaken and desolate" (Matt. 23:37–38). This seems to be a prophecy of the destruction that is to come upon the city in the not too distant future and probably should be read together with other texts to the same effect. It shows again that Jesus' own lament, concern, and distress are not for himself but for his people.

And it reminds us that salvation is not only of the individual but of the community, of the world. Our consciousness transformation must be such that it can transform the way we live in communities from the footwashing model to the Holy Communion model. Only so can we build the true Jerusalem, the City of Peace. The city of Jesus' day was in serious danger at the time when he spoke, and in fact the city was destroyed by the Romans in 70 C.E. and the Jewish people scattered. Foreseeing this, Jesus had cause to mourn. We are in a similar situation — and no doubt every age sees itself in the traditional prophecies and feels that the portentous words point directly to its case. We are still acutely aware of what *could* happen to the planet if an accident or some madman triggered a nuclear holocaust. But we are becoming increasing aware of what actually *is* happening to the planet because of ignorance, carelessness, selfishness, and greed. Ranchers and developers are destroying the rain forests; waste gases are destroying the ozone layer and also creating a greenhouse effect; even the oceans are beginning to succumb to pollution; hazardous wastes have no place to rest and are continuing to accumulate. And so on. Meanwhile, our populations increase and our appetites for energy and advanced technologies grow apace. All this in addition to the usual squabbles among human beings over who shall control what land and what people, what resources and what markets.

The lesson for us is that at this stage in our spiritual development we must again take seriously our obligations to the community, to the large-scale activities of the human race. Spiritual life is often an excuse for extreme privacy, for defaulting and checking out from the common life of the world. This station teaches us that that won't do, that's not the idea. God did not speak his creative Word only to have it return to him void. The world does not exist as something to be forsaken by us. Our spiritual life is hypocritical unless we open it to a realistic concern for the whole world. Realistic concern means that we must not simply *say* that we care, but we must *do* something to contribute to the salvation of the world.

This is moving very close to the paradigm of Holy Communion now, the goal of our transformation. The central concern of our spiritual life begins to shift, or to open up and expand, so that our desire for our own salvation — whatever we may mean by that — stretches to desire for the salvation of the whole world. Our mood grows to coincide with that of Jesus when he says, "I have come that you may have life and have it abundantly!" A sincere will for abundant life for all grows in us at this stage. Remember the image of Holy Communion as everyone feeding every other one and sharing in a common life. This means that we have to think very carefully about ethnic, political, religious, and national separations and loyalties. We have to think about the preciousness of diversity and variety and freedom, together with unity and wholeness and mutual involvement. We may want to reconsider whether the categories of "competitor" and "adversary" are really desirable categories that we want to keep. There are hard problems in this area. Human psychology has to be understood and allowed for. We can err as badly by overestimating it as by underestimating it. It does evolve. We are capable of social insights and feelings now that people in former ages could not begin to comprehend. And our evolution is continuing. Our job is to try to gauge it correctly. Trying to force sharing on people psychologically unprepared for it results in dictatorship, which is worse than not sharing. But encouraging selfishness impedes our development as a community. The lesson of this station is that our spiritual vocation includes concerns on this level. We are not excused from applying ourselves in some way to these problems.

In fact, we realize at this stage that we ourselves cannot traverse this path, cannot complete this journey, unless our motivation is not our own salvation but the salvation of the whole world. Otherwise, we separate ourselves off, turn our attention inward upon ourselves alone, focus all our spiritual energies on our single self, to the exclusion and neglect of all others. This is to cast ourselves into "outer darkness, where there is weeping and gnashing of teeth." This is the inherent danger of the spiritual life, and we must constantly guard against it. Trying to live a spiritual life can be a great temptation to even greater egoism than we had to begin with; it can separate us more, make us feel more isolated. So we need to understand and accept that to be a disciple of Christ is to concern ourselves with the sinful world, to take our share of carrying it, to give ourselves for its welfare and fullness of life. The more we realize that we do share in the divine life, the more we will see that we must be like Christ, who did not consider divinity something to be clung to, but emptied himself into the world, there to be its food and drink.

The Ninth Station: Jesus Falls the Third Time

We now approach those mysteries that are truly mysterious, in the sense that they pass beyond the usual forms of our understanding. One feels that the ascent becomes very steep at this point. Strange reversals take place and paradoxes are pressed into service in the effort to put spiritual reality into words. We are coming close to the mystical, properly so called, the time of self-loss and transformation.

The form that the failure to open completely to divine grace takes at this point—the form that we are now sensitive enough to become aware of — is a very curious form. It is the form of "striving," of "trying," of putting forth efforts. Effort has been necessary up till now. Trying was proof of our sincerity. We could not unify ourselves without this work on our part to do this, stop that, let go of the other, give here, accept there, and so on. Now our eyes open to see that God's grace is fully available to us here and now, in the present moment, and that it is both folly and falsehood to think of it as separated from us by time, off in the future somewhere, or separated from us in any other way.

We had been thinking of ourselves as the Prodigal Son, separated from his father and wasting his life. Then he "comes to himself," as the story says, and sets out on his return journey home. And now, suddenly, just as home is in sight, the scene shifts to the older brother, who had been at home all along, and to our surprise we find ourselves in his role. We are startled to find that we have been living with the Father all the time; there is no separation. We are able now to hear the Father saying to us, "Son, you are always with me, and all that is mine is yours."

We realize that both of these brothers are in us. Even when we begin to understand that we are living with the Father now and always, we still cast ourselves in the role of the separated child, struggling to get back. Or, when we think that we never left home, we may still want something a little extra: a kid to make merry with our friends — as if being with our Father and knowing that all that is his is ours were not enough. It is hard for us to give up *desiring*, to give up striving, to give up struggling, to give up being dissatisfied. We have been taught that we should never be satisfied, we should always keep trying to be and do better. All right, we understand the context in which that is said and how it is meant. But now we've acquired the habit of it, and we find it hard to give up.

We can't imagine what it would be like not to struggle, not to strive, not to desire. And that's part of the "fallenness" of this station. Our self-image is still functioning as one that desires and strives, and we are still clinging to that self-image. Even when we understand that the "trying" to attain our spiritual goal is precisely an impediment to realizing its attainment, because it presupposes — contrary to fact — that it is not "at hand," even then we cannot relinquish trying: we begin to try to not-try.

Jesus speaks to this condition in us when he explains how he himself views his own work. Jesus works, and yet it is as though he does not work. He describes it this way: "Truly, truly, I tell you, the Son can do nothing of his own accord, but only what he sees the Father doing; for whatever he does, that the Son does likewise. For the Father loves the Son, and shows him all that he himself is doing" (John 5:19–20). Does this sound like what the father in the Prodigal Son story says to the older brother? Again he says, "I can do nothing on my own authority" (John 5:30); "but the Father who dwells in me does the works" (John 14:10).

But for this paradoxical doing/not-doing to characterize us, we have to be totally open and available. Trying to succeed at the "spiritual life" and being disappointed when we fail, discriminating between success and failure, watching and judging ourselves — all this prevents us from being fully open and available. We are still occupied with ourselves and our own perfection. Strange as it sounds, we have — at this stage, not earlier — to stop trying to "be good" or to concern ourselves in any way with the merits or otherwise of our own lives. This is where the "way" gets "narrow"; some have likened it to a razor's edge: it is so easy to fall off on the side either of trying too much or of not trying enough. It is a peculiar balance and abandonment that is required.

Living takes place only in the present. Not in the past and not in the future. The God Jesus knows and preaches is "the God of the living, not of the dead." Both the past and the future are nonliving. Only the present is alive and real. It is out of the realization of this truth that Jesus gives voice to those great utterances that include the holy name I AM. "I AM the Way, the Truth, and the Life"; "I AM the living bread that came down from heaven"; "I AM the resurrection"; "I AM the light of the world." And so on.

We may have read these passages mainly in terms of whatever titles followed the words "I AM," but I would draw your attention to the "I AM" itself. It affirms the act of existing, being, living, at the present moment. Now. Here. Jesus emphasized it when he declared, "Before Abraham was, I AM" (John 8:58). And Abraham is an important figure: the Father of all that follows, like a cause in the ancient past. Jesus, however, not only antedates all causal sequences, but is now in a way that transcends time itself.

Right now, in the present moment, I AM is available to us, is in us, is making us to be. Unless we recognize this fact, says Jesus, we are still lost; we're not in touch with reality yet. "You will die in your sins unless you believe that I AM" (John 8:24).

This is the same message with which Jesus began his ministry: "Repent, for the kingdom of heaven is at hand" (Matt. 4:17). Not distant and not delayed, but present, available. It is, in fact, within us (Luke 17:21). We are not to be looking around for it, seeking it in this place or that.

There is a secret in this, as is stressed by three evangelists (Matt. 13:11; Mark 4:11; Luke 8:10), something that is not easy to grasp. It is the open secret that we may not understand even if we hear it. But the more we begin to understand it, the more it will open up to us and we will know it better still — "To him who has, more shall be given." At a certain point we realize that the kingdom of God in us doesn't require any effort on our part: "The kingdom of God is as if a man should scatter seed upon the ground, and should sleep and rise night and day, and the seed should sprout and grow, he knows not how. The earth produces of itself" (Mark 4:26–27).

This availability of the divine kingdom is the Good News. All we have to do is relinquish our barriers against it, and it is fully present.

— Seven —

THE DEATH OF THE WORD

❦

WE ARE NOW ENTERING into the mystical night, the night in which "no man can work" (John 9:4), in which the operations of human nature are transcended, in which the last vestiges of the isolated self fade away. The central idea here is that the mystical death is the death of all concepts and the abandoning of the position in consciousness that generates and processes concepts. This is the Word level in us, that which "exegetes" and interprets all our experience. John 1:18 acknowledges this exegeting function as a unique offspring of the invisible God, our Ground, Source, "Father." Nevertheless, at this point in our spiritual development, it is to our advantage that the Exegete be withdrawn, for otherwise the Holy Spirit — the immanent presence of God within us, the subjective, interior reality as distinguished from the objective or exterior, projected interpretation — cannot rise up within us as our primary consciousness (John 16:7).

In the preceding chapter I used the Stations of the Cross as metaphors for stages in our spiritual journey, and we had gone as far as the Ninth Station, leaving three more to the Twelfth, where our interior interpretation of these pictures ends. In this chapter I will make use of images related to these last three stations, but without dividing the material exactly in their sequence. And there will be further explanations of the role of the Word and of our state of consciousness when it is withdrawn.

116

Also, it will become clear why "human nature" cannot "work" in the last moments and how the Holy Spirit appears.

Nakedness and Invisibility

I think we ought to remind ourselves as we begin this final leg in the journey toward divine Emptiness that, although the traditional imagery is couched in terms of "death," we are really always advancing toward greater life. Everything we are doing is "good for us"; it is something we want to do. We can also say that we are moving toward wider and deeper truth from the lesser and limited truths with which we began.

At this point we will be relieved to find the isolated self fading away. The isolated self is the self that believes itself to be separate and set apart from others because it has clothed itself in descriptions in order to give itself an appearance of distinction. Thomas Merton speaks of what he calls the "false self" in this way:

> I wind experiences around myself and cover myself with pleasures and glory like bandages in order to make myself perceptible to myself and to the world, as if I were an invisible body that could only become visible when something visible covered its surface.[1]

At this stage in our spiritual journey these coverings and disguises are stripped from us — or we shed them. You might say that the "real self" then shows. Or, you might say that what is revealed is indeed the invisibility that is at our core. And saying that, you might remember that God is invisible, and that we are children of God.

What does invisibility mean? We are equating it here with nakedness, and both of them with reality. It means not being identified with descriptions. I see this as the crucial point in our transformation, our metamorphosis or emergence into the adult

form of our life. It is because we identify ourselves with our social descriptions that we set ourselves apart from one another,
feel the need to defend and augment ourselves, and organize our
societies in terms of domination patterns. When we suddenly (or
even slowly) see that all these fine clothes are as unreal as the
emperor's, a fundamental shift occurs in our consciousness. The
sense of who we are, where we stand, from where we look out,
moves back a long way, so that our perspective changes enormously and our sense of identification becomes as wide as our
"visual field" has become.

We had been identifying with the ego-self, the one with the
particular collection of descriptions that we and those who
know us identify as our unique human reality. All those descriptions are significant by their distinction from the descriptions
from which they differ, the ways of being that they are not. The
differences are what make these descriptions of ourselves visible,
and the visibility is what makes us believe that they are real. We
know who we are (we believe) by being able to tell ourselves
apart from other beings. And for its own proper purposes this
is a perfectly good way of organizing our workaday world. It is
only when we are seriously in quest of the deepest reality that
we realize that for that purpose these "clothes" might as well
not be there. We know that *we* are not that.

It becomes clear that we had been investing quantities of
attention and personal energy in maintaining these significant
differences so that we could feel our own reality in contrast to
our neighbor's. And by that very token, of course, we had to
prefer our welfare and advantage (from some point of view,
even that of excelling in obedience or self-sacrifice) to those
of others. That kept us isolated, separated, and on edge, pro-
tective, watchful for our security in this descriptive-difference
kind of reality. It was not possible to love our neighbor as being an extension of our self. Our selfhood stopped where our
neighbor's began.

Now we see that that very notion of who and what we are,
that concern for defending that kind of selfhood, is what has

made it so hard to love and share and care equally and what has kept us so exhausted by the quantities of energy the defense and advancement always required. There was never any relaxation; the more "goods" of wealth or honor or virtue we gathered to ourselves, the more we had to protect, the greater our losses could be. And our very dissatisfaction, our pain of worry, our tension and tiredness, at length enable us to see that we, the real we, are not these descriptions.

The "I" that sees this, that sees through the descriptive clothes and stands back from the descriptions, is another level of selfhood, assumes another perspective, and sees relations differently. It has moved into a certain kind of invisibility and relates to others in terms of their corresponding invisibility. The outstanding characteristic of this shift is that our former privileged point of view, looking at everything from the standpoint of our personal ego-self, has disappeared. Our "standpoint" is now expanded, spread over the whole. Every "other" is now counted as part of "self."

We can try to force ourselves to behave in "unselfish" ways, and we can also recognize and cultivate our instincts of empathy, fellow-feeling, and sharing. But the important spiritual step that takes place at this stage in our development is a radical seeing-through of a whole way of organizing and valuing the world of experience. The goods of pleasure, wealth, honor, and virtue suddenly become irrelevant. The feeling is that they "drop away" from us. We are no longer energetically interacting with them, they no longer move us, motivate us. The faculties, the functions of our consciousness and behavior, that had been engaged with those issues and goals are said to be "fasting." They are no longer being fed by our attention and interest and spiritual drive.

This spiritual drive had been making a closed loop: reaching out, grasping a "good," and pulling it into the ego-self. Part of what made that experience a "good" was that we got it instead of someone else. That contrast was essential to the sense of value and in turn confirmed our sense of our separated self. This sort of spiritual drive can be called *eros,* the love that seeks the benefit of the lover. Through its energy all this universe has been built up and we ourselves as conscious persons have created societies and culture and technology. We have even developed religion and a certain advancement in spirituality on its basis. To seek the "salvation of one's soul" is an erotic quest.

But now there is a fundamental shift. All these benefits to the ego-self are insufficient. And the ego-self, no matter how well benefitted, is insufficient. Our central spiritual drive exceeds that type of reality. It wills something larger. It wills the being, the more-being, the better-being, of the whole. Since the whole is perceived as being a community of unique beings, this is simultaneously a will to the benefit of each singular being in a direct and "personal" way. The feeling is that energy goes out from us to enter into the other and nurture the other. It does not intend to return to us, benefitting us.

We may remember some biblical images of this. Noah, on the verge of entering the new world after the flood, sent out a dove. The first two times she returned to him, the second time with an olive leaf. But the third time he sent her forth, "she did not return to him any more" (Gen. 8:9–12). The development of our conscious spiritual drive may be said to resemble this. Another image is Jesus, who, having been "touched" in a special way by one who sought healing from him, reported that he felt "that power had gone forth from him" (Mark 5:30). The power did not return to him but remained in the one who had touched him and brought about the desired healing. We may also notice that this occurs while Jesus is on his way to effect a passage from death to life by raising the daughter of Jairus.

This movement of spiritual power is called agape, the love that seeks the benefit of the beloved. It is the movement of the deeper self, with its larger scope and truer action. It does not intend to protect or improve the descriptions of the lover. It intends to share basic being with the whole community, each unique being in the community, impartially, equally. This is the love that God is, by which sun and rain are sent to the good and the evil alike, to both the just and the unjust (Matt. 5:45). This is the model for love, the essential spiritual drive, the movement of, or toward, perfection. It is revealed to us that this is our essential self; we are to be like this, "perfect, as your heavenly Father is perfect" (Matt. 5:48).

Notice that agape is not motivated by the descriptions of the beloved — good, evil, just, unjust. Nor does it arise from some local and contrasting description of a lover who sizes up the world as composed of "friends and enemies." What would be "enemies" in the view of an ego-self and its eros-drive are to be loved just the same as "friends." In other words, those categories don't apply; this lover is not an ego-self. Both lover and beloved have been stripped of their descriptions and united in their spiritual nakedness.

But "each" is "all," and the God that is the agape is "all in all" (1 John 4:8; 1 Cor. 15:28). This is how and why agape reaches the whole. There are no limiting descriptions dividing the lovers. They are all "naked"; they are all "invisible." There is no contrast among them, some being acceptable and others not. There is nothing to be defended, nor anything to gain. We are no longer "measuring" ourselves and one another. We are no longer "judging" (Matt. 7:1), especially not by "appearances" (John 7:24).

The Dark Night of the Soul

This stage is sometimes called "the dark night of the soul." That expression doesn't mean some kind of depression or sorrow or despair, though it does represent a kind of crisis in the sense of a very fundamental shift in consciousness. It is a parallel to "the dark night of the senses" and means that those faculties have, so to speak, turned off. Significant information no longer comes to us from our sense life when we cease building our lives around sense experiences. This is what happens in the early days of the spiritual journey, when the accent of our major interest shifts from the pleasures of the senses to the affairs of the spirit. We are no longer "turned on" in terms of our senses, although they continue, of course, in a normal healthful way and in terms of serious esthetic experience. But we are not building our lives around the elementary levels of sense pleasures. It is in that regard that they are in "darkness." Eating and drinking and sex and money and power are no longer Number One in our lives. We can enjoy and use them modestly and righteously, but they are not the most important things in our lives.

The "dark night of the soul," or better, of the mind, is analogous to the dark night of the senses, but is said of the mental faculties instead of the bodily faculties. We are talking about our ways of knowing and planning, desiring and willing. We are confronting the ultimate question of meaning — finding out what is and what its value is. We are asking what, after all, is the meaning of our lives: who are we in essence, and what is the worth of our being and our doing? And the deeper we probe this question area, the closer we come to the point where our usual ways of answering such questions no longer work. And the basic reason for this is not that our minds are weak — although that is true, too — but that the "answer" cannot be put in the terms in which our "minds" operate. Our instruments and methods are no longer able to illuminate the subject matter on which our attention is focused. In that sense the mental faculties are also in "darkness."

Because we had shifted from identifying primarily with our bodies and their sense pleasures and pains, we are at this stage strongly identifying with our minds, their ideas and feelings and intentions. And it has probably not yet occurred to us that this identification may not yet be the bottommost real self, either. Therefore we continue to struggle with our ideas and arguments, our energies of valuing and dedicating ourselves, our goal-seeking, hoping to find among these activities and the sorts of realities to which they are addressed the ultimate answer, the final meaning of life. But the arguments, the principles, the definitions, the values, the purposes, the goals, all seem to develop counterexamples, failures to cover everything, to answer all objections. Most of all, they leave room for further questioning, and since we had asked for a final and unquestionable answer, we find ourselves getting deeper and deeper into doubt.

Doubt means "doubling," doubling of the mind: looking for an explanation of the mind (and its experiences) by means of the mind. What is an "explanation"? Doesn't it mean to account for something not understood by deriving it from what is understood, from something more primitive, more foundational, ultimately, from something self-evident, something about which we are not inclined to raise any question? But when we ask, What is the purpose of life? we do not come to such an end. If the purpose of my life is to rear my children, then shall I not ask what *their* purpose is? Or if I say my purpose is to reduce suffering in the world, shall I not ask what the purpose of the world shall be after we have eliminated its sufferings? Or if we deem that unlikely, what is the purpose of having a suffering world that we endlessly try to set right? Why have a finite world at all? When we have eliminated from our own concerns and goals the correction of local defects and the attainment of personal comfort, these global questions expand before us.

Sometimes such questions are answered by saying it is all for the glorification of God. But is this an "explanation"? Reframing the mysterious in terms of the clear? Hardly. And at this point the familiar religious "explanations" or accounts suddenly seem puerile, like ancient stories told to primitive people hardly able to think deeply on anything. Nothing makes sense. We cannot trust any of the old teachers. Nobody really knows. We are here, in this enormous universe, at the mercy of all sorts of "elements," full of unfulfilled desires and facing final frustration, no matter how many local satisfactions we might achieve. We don't see what it is all for, nor why it couldn't have been arranged more pleasantly. We have consciousness, and consciousness cries out for understanding and for a feeling that its efforts are for a worthy attainment, but when all temporal achievements are

seen to be finally perishing, no understanding or satisfaction is
in sight.

This is the mind trying to satisfy itself by means of the mind,
in the terms of the mind, and it is like being nailed to the cross,
struggling first one way and then another to relieve the pain
a little. The contradictions and paradoxes are inescapable, no
matter how we twist.

But this is salutary, for it alerts us to the fact that what we
seek cannot be found this way. Why can it not? Because we are
looking for an explanation and a meaning that would be *outside*
ourselves as seekers, and because we are using concepts, which
have finite forms limited by their relations to one another. Just
as we had to give up descriptions, so now we have to abandon
concepts and forms. The Ultimate must be the Absolute, the Unconditioned. It cannot be captured or accounted for in terms of
relative concepts of conditioned forms. No amount of cleverness
on our part can achieve that. The Ultimate cannot be "known"
that way. This is the full meaning of the "invisibility" of God.
The attempt to know by concepts and forms means that we are
trying to "look at" God, thus making God relative to ourselves.
But, of course, that wouldn't then be God.

Much less is it sufficient or satisfactory to suppose that we
can replace knowledge by "faith." Certainly we cannot do it
by "faith" in the sense of taking the word of others, whether
persons or institutions, as they expound a doctrine, account, or
explanation. Nor can it be done by "faith" in the sense of giving up seeking for the time being and just trusting that "it will
all turn out all right": there must be a meaning, but we can't
understand it now. Both of these claim that meaning has to be
"revealed," as though the trouble was with the subject matter
to be known. The trouble is deeper than that, and in this context "revealing" won't help any. Both of these kinds of "faith"
still assume that the meaning is expressible in concepts. It is not.
That's the point.

What we are seeking (and if we are real, we cannot give
up seeking) cannot be known about, known as an object —

a "knowable" — is known by a subject, a knower. It cannot
be known from the outside, as something set over against us,
which we are not. Therefore, to fulfill our seeking — and to
fulfill the scriptural promise "Seek, and you will find" (Matt.
7:7) — we must continue to press forward in the line of knowledge, but go beyond knowing relatively, knowing by means of
concepts, knowing as subject knows object, knowing from the
outside. We must pass to what Meister Eckhart called "princip-
ial knowledge," from *within* the Ultimate, the Unconditioned
Principle:

> There is a principle in the intellective soul, untouched by
> time and corporeality.... In this principle is God,... ever
> flowering in all the fullness and glory of his actual Self....
> It is free of all names and void of all structures. It is one
> and unconditioned, as God is one and unconditioned, and
> no [one] can in any way behold it mentally.[2]

Yet mental life is what has brought us to this critical stage, has
nurtured our spirituality and lifted us from step to higher step.
The formation of concepts and their representation by linguistic
symbols[3] is what has made human life transcendently superior
to all the other forms of life on this planet. It is in humanity that
"the Word" has become incarnate. It is through "the Word"
that all our world is created and known. Only when symbolization has come to hold the primacy in our conscious life does
our experience become an organized "universe." And it is only
through "the Word" that we come to approach the Source, the
Ultimate. And yet, at the very end, "the Word" has to "die," to
be withdrawn, to be passed beyond. This seems most strange, to
give up the very best thing we have, our "Isaac," our only hope
for continuance into the future.

But the Word says of itself, "The Father is greater than I,"
and that if we valued it properly, we would rejoice in its withdrawal into the bosom of the Father (John 14:28B), for this is
the rightful career of the Word. There is a nonconceptual domain prior to concepts, of which the world of the Word is an

explicitation (John 1:18). The Word comes out of this original reality, foundational Being, and as it comes makes the world for the children of the Word, the concept-users. But there is also a domain *beyond* the world of concepts, conscious realization of foundational existence, of the Root of Being, and the Word fulfills and finishes its work (John 17:4; 19:28, 30) in leading consciousness to the state that is beyond.

This is the hardest struggle and the greatest doubt. We face having to give up our particular worldview, our culture, our ideas about how things are, ultimately our God-concept. All of this makes us feel as if God has abandoned us. Who — what — shall we be, if we cease operating in terms of ideas and cultural allegiances, that is to say, if we cease identifying ourselves as this being here who is known as the one who operates in terms of these ideas and cultural forms? After all, we are a magnificent being, capable of detached, critical thought and appraisal, able to stand apart from nature and analyze it. And following on this, we think that we can stand apart from God and analyze the ways of God with the world.

But we can't. Not because God is so superior to us, but because we cannot *stand apart from* God. We are not *outside,* able to look on. We are *inside,* not "looking on" at all, but actively *being* that reality which we thought to "know."

That the Spirit May Come

"I tell you the truth: it is to your advantage that I go away, for if I do not go away, the Paraclete will not come to you; but if I go, I will send him to you" (John 16:7). The projecting, exegeting Word has to go away in order to permit our vision to turn inward, to become in-sight into the reality that we ourselves are. As long as the eyes of our mind are turned outward, that is, toward that which (we suppose) we *are not,* so long will we be unable to be aware of the Spirit within, that which we essentially *are,* "a spring of water welling up to eternal life" (John

4:14). We must not "continue to cling to" the Word, but allow it to be thoroughly withdrawn back into the Father (John 20:17).

We ourselves are thus drawn back into our center, into our Spirit, into that whose origin and destination are unknown and unknowable and that is free to move wherever it wills (John 3:8). This is our reality; we are "born of the Spirit," that is to say, we are Spirit. We cannot project this reality before us and "examine" it. We "know" it by being it.

Notice that we are no longer trying to bring our body and mind into correct behavior. Compared with Spirit, they are both on the side of "flesh," which "is of no avail" for "eternal life" (John 6:27, 54, 63). Trying to improve body and mind by means of body and mind produces only more body and mind: "That which is born of the flesh is flesh." Only "that which is born of the Spirit is Spirit" (John 3:6). We have to enter into a domain that transcends both body and mind, "transcends" in the way a third dimension transcends the two dimensions of a surface. You will never get to the moon by traveling farther and farther on the face of the earth. You have to go up, at right angles to both length and width.

Similarly, Spirit forsakes both ends of any polarity. Where body-and-mind feel obliged to choose one and reject the other, Spirit answers, "None of the above." This is what Jesus said to the Samaritan woman who questioned him about worshiping the way the Samaritans do or the way the Jews do: "Neither." Spirit and truth aren't items in an array of competitors. To get to the truth and the Spirit, you have to go beyond the world in which you choose one way in preference to another. We enter a consciousness in which the old dualisms no longer apply. This is what was foreshadowed already in the Sermon on the Mount, where all dualisms are indicated by those deep-seated dualisms of "the just and the unjust," "the good and the evil," "friend and enemy." In the perfection of God, the difference between them is obliterated. But if we retain the distinction, then the Holy Spirit cannot come up in our interior. That mode of mental operation has to cease, to die.

It is helpful to remember and to stress that we are talking about a shift in viewpoint and in the sense of self-identity. We are rising above the privileged (chosen) particular viewpoint and are identifying with the whole, with the perfection of God. Our consciousness, like the Word of God, had to become incarnate in some particularity in order to become incarnate at all. But at this advanced stage of the spiritual endeavor, that particularity itself has to be surpassed or abandoned. It has to die in order that still another and more real, more Godlike, consciousness can be ours. Particularity is replaced by universality or wholeness, and even by the Transcendent, the Absolute. And that means that everything that had been viewed as outside oneself, and known by contrast through being symbolized and represented by a "sacrament," now comes inside and is known by *being it* directly, by immediate possession of the reality itself, not an image of it.

All sacraments are a kind of "language." They function as what we may call "transitive communication," truth being passed from one to another through some medium, some mediator. Now the Mediator dies. This means that our sense of our central Self passes to a deeper place, into the Source ("Father"), and is present to all reality by *intransitive communion,* unmediated, direct, existential. We are no longer knowing by means of representation in a language, but we are in touch with reality itself, at the center where all things arise in God. All our languages, all our sacraments, have brought us to this stage and have now "commended" us into the care of God the Source. We experience ourselves as boundless, beginningless, endless, unaccountable, unconditioned. This is "eternal life," life that is free of the limitations of finite existence.

We know ourselves as children of God. But we know it so well that we "unknowingly forget" it. When the children of God are genuinely children of God, there is no need for them to be conscious that they are children of God.[4] You only think of being children of God when there is an alternative, something to contrast it with, when it could be otherwise. Only then is a flag, a label, a concept, a word necessary. In this central, unitive consciousness, there is no contrast, no alternative, no question, no distance and distinction between subject and object, between that which knows and that which is known. That is why I called it "intransitive communion." Intransitive verbs don't take objects. Communion doesn't reach *across* to another as "communication" does. Here all is unitive as the Persons of the Trinity: each in each. This is what is achieved by the death of the Word.

Let me repeat that the death of which I am speaking takes place *in us*. And it has not successfully taken place until the standpoint from which our consciousness lives is "wholly within God and not as one in direction toward God."[5] That is the difference. The God whom you sought has "suddenly come to his temple" (Mal. 3:1) — which is *you* — and cannot be thought of as outside any longer, as something "toward" which you could turn, as something separate from yourself. Your entire being is "inside" God, and the only God there is is "inside" you. God is not an object for you, and you are not an object for God.

When projection and symbolization and the dualism of subject/object cease — "die" — then "we" are "reconciled" to the Unconditioned, the Unobjectifiable, because we also are unconditioned and not objectifiable. This is original glory, which God gives to all his children, in love, "before the foundation of the world" (John 17:24).

Exercises

1. Go back now to that list of descriptions you made out in the very beginning. Check over them and see if you have been stripped of identification with any of them. Have your attachments to them weakened? Can you feel your own reality without necessarily expressing it in those terms? Continue to center yourself in your spiritual heart, independent of your descriptions. Feel how this gives you a wider life, not isolating you

within the boundaries of your particular "self-description." You do not have to refuse understanding or sympathy with any other by saying "That doesn't fall within my self-description" (as though there were a "job description" for the job of being you).

2. Check to see if your sense of belonging to a group distinguished from other groups is any less than when you began Lent. Give yourself permission to feel that you *belong* to the widest possible "group" — everything that lives in God. Don't insist on identifying by belonging to a specialized subgroup (race, gender, church, political party, economic class, etc.).

3. Are you doing less of sorting the relationships in your life into superior/inferior, dominant/submissive, good/bad, friends/enemies? Baptism is going to return us to the state of Paradise, before we thought dividing things into all sorts of pairs of opposites was a smart thing to do. The vows we renew spell out our consent to live with this unified outlook. Take another look at the form of renewal (e.g., "Will you strive for justice and peace among all people and respect the dignity of every human being?").

4. Can you feel the freedom of the "invisible" self? Loosening the descriptions, widening the boundaries, being "naked" is supposed to make you feel free and expansive and real and happy. You do not have to pretend; you do not have to defend. You can just be, just live.

5. As you feel this freedom and its happiness, notice that quite spontaneously "virtue goes out from you." You seem to be quietly radiating good will to the world at large. You are not pushing it. It just happens. You just naturally "glow." You can't help smiling; you can't help loving and creating.

6. This love that goes out from you without your having to push it pays no attention to the descriptions of those it shines on. It is quite independent of them. It sees that somehow its reality, radiant unconditional love, is what everything is made of, deep down.

7. This doesn't match too well with sense observation or with our usual ideas about experience and the world. But we

are beginning to stand in another space now, where we perceive with another faculty, one that senses the presence of God in unlikely places. We do not have to explain it; we directly perceive it. This is what is properly called "faith." We perceive it directly because we ourselves are in it; it is in us. We are *doing* it. We are *being* it. The real presence of God is no longer an object in front of us. It is what we ourselves are and are doing. It is this radiance that comes forth from us effortlessly and unites with the radiances from all other beings. Sit for a time in this realization and then carry it with you.

— Eight —

THE GREAT SABBATH

═══════════════ ❦ ═══════════════

OUR LITURGICAL PRACTICE is designed to show us the day following Good Friday as a day of nothingness. In the liturgical churches the altars are stripped; the reservation tabernacles are empty and their doors stand ajar; there is no ceremony until late in the night. From the time that the Word is withdrawn at the ninth hour on Friday until it reappears on Easter morning, there is a great hush, a great silence, a great pause, as though nothing moves and all nature holds its breath.

What does this powerful Nothingness mean? For it is meaningful, exceedingly meaningful. It is not just a matter of "waiting." This is a high symbol, indeed the symbol to which everything else has led. All the exercises of Lent, all the concentration of Holy Week, all the final abandonments of Good Friday are intended to bring us to this Great Nothing. It is our way of pointing to that which cannot be said; this is why the Word is gone. There is no object outside us on which we may fasten. Nothing to observe, nothing happening, nothing to do. Our usual, finite, comparative, means-to-end activity is suspended. We are in the presence of the Infinite; we are in fact *in* the Infinite.

In the Bosom of the Father

There are many feasts in the Christian calendar for God the Son and a great festival, Pentecost, for God the Holy Spirit. But there is no feast of God the Father. Isn't this strange? So perhaps we may regard Holy Saturday, the day of Sacred Nothingness, as commemorative of God the Father, the Formless, the Infinite.

There is a strong apophatic tradition in Christian theology, especially in the theology of the Eastern church; less well-known is the apophatic tradition in Judaism. Devotion to the Hidden God and to the Sacred Nothingness appears in Jewish mysticism. The thirteenth-century Spanish Kabbalist, Isaac the Blind, for instance, developed a contemplative mysticism leading to communion with God through meditation on the divine attributes (*sefirot*) and the heavenly essences (*havayot*). At the head of the world of divine qualities he put the "thought," from which emerged the divine utterances, the "words" by which the world was created. But above the thought is the Hidden God, the Infinite. The way of the mystic is to ascend from words — all of which ultimately derive from one source, the divine name — to be absorbed in the divine Thought.[1]

Kabbalistic mystics also point to the "realm which no created being can intellectually comprehend" by saying that "God Who is called *Ein-Sof* (without end, Infinite) in respect of himself is called *Ayin* (Nothingness) in respect of his first self-revelation." Some of them regarded this Absolute Nothingness as the Source from which all things emerged. Certainly it was a full and powerful Nothingness. David b. Abraham (end of the thirteenth century) defined the *Ayin* as "having more being than any other being in the world, but since it is simple [one], and all other simple things are complex [composed unities] when compared with its simplicity, so in comparison it is called 'nothing.' " And it is further said that "if all the powers returned to Nothingness, the Primeval One who is the cause of all would remain in unity without distinctions in the depths of nothingness."[2]

Often people who have gone into the wilderness speak of

"hearing the silence." When I go into the empty church on Holy Saturday (before the ceremonies of the Easter Vigil, which should take place well into the night) and experience the Holy Nothingness "reverberating," as it were, on all sides, it seems to me that we have here a powerful pointer to — a "sacrament," a mystery of — the Primeval One, whose Word has returned into itself, whose manifestation is not now projected, whose self-revelation is gathered into its own essential unity for the timeless moment of the Great Sabbath. It is the day sacred to the very Source itself, from which all manifestation derives:

> Every good gift and every perfect gift is from above, coming down from the Father of lights with whom there is no variation or shadow due to change. Of his own will he brought us forth by the word of truth that we should be a kind of first fruits of his creatures. (James 1:17–18)

This is the coming forth. The Sabbath represents the return and the resting in the bosom of the Source, the original unity (John 13:1, 3; 3:13; 1:18), the return to the Hidden One.

The Sabbath means rest and is distinguished from work, from labor. "Labor" is what we have been doing up to this point, working on ourselves, letting God "work" in us. At this point we cease from labor. St. Teresa likens the spiritual life to various modes of watering a garden, most of them involving some kind of effort on our part. But in the end, she says, no effort is necessary, for God sends the rain. The paradox is that our effort, our labor, has been contributory toward bringing us into this life-giving rain. We can even put it this way: we have labored at learning how to cease laboring. Learning how to stop is a central concern in the meditation heart of the spiritual life.

And yet our "ceasing" does not cause the Sabbath to come. Rather, we cease because the "work" is completed, because we have gone as far as we can by that means and have been carried past that point into God's Sabbath. We can notice that Jesus declares that he has "finished" the work his Father gave him to do (John 17:4; cf. 19:30) and that both Acts (21:7) and

2 Timothy (4:7) speak of "finishing one's course." We can also consider that these are images of God's work in creation and God's resting when the work was finished:

> And on the seventh day God finished the work that he had done, and he rested on the seventh day from all the work that he had done. So God blessed the seventh day and hallowed it. (Gen. 2:2–3)

The Sabbath that we keep in an outward way is a "sacrament" of the real Sabbath, indicated in these texts. That it is such a sign was said already in the Book of Exodus:

> You shall keep my sabbaths, for this is a sign between me and you throughout your generations, given in order that you may know that I, the Lord, sanctify you. (Exod. 31:13)

That we may know that God sanctifies us, makes us holy, brings us into the divine life itself: this is what we are trying to realize, to have vividly and foundationally in our consciousness. This "sanctification" is spoken of in the present tense. It is not something coming later on, at some time in the future. It is what is. But the awareness of it was covered over, and we were distracted from it. We have been working — God has been working — to draw our attention from the distractions, to "dis-cover" this primal reality of our being to us.

Someone has said that "prayer is the work of God within us."[3] If this is so, then the union with the Father in the Great Sabbath is "the leisure of God within us." Leisure is a wonderful concept when it is considered as one way of expressing this Sabbath of God. We can notice that it is not at all the same thing as "idleness," a failure to act due to lassitude, lack of "heart" for the work. That kind of not-working comes from failure to affirm the reality and goodness of one's own being as born from God. It is inability to make an effort in the line of confidence in this God-born being and paradoxically often leads to frenetic activity and "workaholism" to drown out the pain of this lack of true being. Leisure, on the other hand, is not *needing* to make an effort — not needing to, because one is thoroughly aware of one's reality and goodness in God. Divine leisure is neither effort nor idleness. It rejoices on a plane that transcends that of work, whether done or not done.[4]

I think that this is an important idea, that it is *God's* Sabbath that is being celebrated in us as our Sabbath. Our realization of it, of the "rejoicing in heaven" (Luke 15:7, 10), is our living inside God, being nothing but God-life (see John 14:9–10, Gal. 2:20, and 1 John 3:9). The peace that we feel is the peace of God, God's own peacefulness, which surpasses all ordinary understanding (Phil. 4:7, cf. Col. 3:15). Similarly, we share in God's own freedom, happiness, and unity, because by becoming intensely aware that we have received God's own Spirit — by discovering that we are "born of the Spirit" — we find that we are immersed in the "depths of God" (1 Cor. 2:10–11).

Here we pass beyond merely linked multiplicities, synthetic unities, and are in true at-one-ment. We are beyond all dualities. God's leisure is neither effort nor idleness; God's peace is neither agitation nor apathy, enmity nor alliance; God's bliss is neither pleasure nor pain; God's righteousness is neither justice nor injustice; God's knowledge is neither affirmation nor negation, neither ignorance nor understanding; God's reality — or "isness," as Meister Eckhart would say — is neither something nor nothing. Whatever is what it is by comparison is not yet in God's Sabbath. We, as we are in God's Sabbath, are not real or valuable by comparison. We simply are.

Our awareness thus is *within God*. This is our primal, foundational awareness. And whatever knowledge we have of God's manifestation is from within God. This is why and how our consciousness "rests from all the works that it has done." We are no longer to know things from the outside, no longer struggling to be good and possess value as distinguished from being bad and disvalued. We are in the simplicity, the at-one-ment, of *isness*. The graciousness of God transcends all these pairs of opposites, and we find ourselves, *find* our *selves,* in this graciousness. This graciousness is the isness, is what we are, is what everything is. This is "Deus meus — Deus noster — et omnia": my God, our God, everything, all. Not so much that it is a God whom I acknowledge but, much deeper, that it is the God, the Godness that is mine, my own Godness in this universal graciousness.

"This Day..."

"Jesus, remember me when you come into your kingdom." "Truly, I promise you, this day you will be with me in Paradise" (Luke 23:42, 43). "This day" is the Great Sabbath. It is, so to speak, the only day, the day of which all other days are but reflections. The first chapter of John tells how the Baptist pointed out Jesus to two of his disciples, who followed Jesus and asked "where he was staying." They were told, "Come, and you will see." And "they came and saw where he was staying; and they stayed with him that day" (John 1:35–39). That day: they came and they saw and they stayed. They stayed with him.... "Father, I desire that they also...may be with me where I am, to behold my glory, which you have given me in your love for me, before the foundation of the world" (John 17:24). Be "with me where I am" means "stay" with me "where I am staying." And they stayed with him that day.

This is where we are in our spiritual journey. We have come and seen and are now staying, staying with him where he stays, and are beholding his glory, the gift of God, in God's love, before the foundation of the world. When our minds awake in God's Sabbath, this is what happens. We behold the glory of love's giving, as it is, prior to the very foundation of the world. This is why it is a single day. A day out of time altogether.

Furthermore, it is an *available* day, this day — not some other day, some day yet to come, some indefinite day, but this very day. The day of salvation is always "now" (2 Cor. 6:2). In this day of perfect freedom, it is always "now." When we live in perfect freedom, it is always now and always "salvation," and conversely, when we live in "now," we are open to the freedom of salvation. When we stop identifying with the dissatisfaction of what is not yet, stop identifying with goal-seeking behaviors and feelings, the craving for better times, then we become available to the presence of this day. And when our hearts stand still in the perfection of God's love, then we are freed from all cravings and find ourselves alive *now* in God's loving glory, where we are from before the foundation of the world — that is, in eternal life.

Too often our experience of our life is not an experience of gracious glory, unity, and eternity, but of fragmentation; we may, however, be blocking our own vision. For we know that the underlying reality is a continuous wholeness, a unity beyond any possibility of division. This, after all, is part of the insight of monotheism. And one of the ways this wholeness is expressed is as the transcendence of time.

In the personalist context of Judaism this is represented dramatically as God's loyalty, God's steadfastness, as the integrity of God's will. A fragmented will can be loyal one day and defect the next, can change over time. But God's will is integral, utterly reliable, immovable, eternal. It means that God will never forsake us. "His great love is without end" (Ps. 117) and without beginning, that love in which he wraps us in his own glory "before the foundation of the world."

As children of God, we have the right and the capacity to match our wills to God's will by being steadfast, without fluctuation, loyal, committed. If our will is focused in unity, then the rest of our life will be less fragmented. We will gradually draw all back into original unity; we will experience what some Jewish mystics have called "reintegration," the restoration of the world to the wholeness that images the wholeness of God.

The perception of our lives as fragmented is related to our perception of our lives in time. In the first place, there is never enough time, it seems, to accommodate all the tasks we undertake. And in the second place, we make ourselves miserable over this because we value ourselves by what we accomplish. If we suffer in this way, probably our descriptions of ourselves consist of what we have achieved or what we aspire to achieve. This means that we identify ourselves to a great extent with our past or our future, but not with the present. There is not any achievement, or even any description, in the present; it is just being alive, here, now. Whenever we can escape from the past and the future and live in the present, we find that we are not fragmented. Everything comes together in wholeness, because we are not thinking about and evaluating ourselves, but just *being* ourselves.

You can test this by actual experience. By keeping your consciousness quietly and simply in the present moment, you will see that memory and anticipation, guilt and anxiety will disappear. Neither is there any fantasy in a consciousness stayed on the present moment. It has to be perfectly realistic. It is living in the past or in the future that is fantasy, that is unrealistic; we are not in fact living in the past or the future, and our consciousness therefore finds no peace that way. The present moment is the intersection of time with eternity, and when our consciousness is stayed on this, it rests and find peace, because it is released from guilts, anxieties, and fantasies and is in touch with reality.

This is not, of course, to say that we should never think of past or future, that we should not learn from history or make plans for days ahead. Those are obviously appropriate and important things to do, and our ability to do them is one of the marvels of our consciousness. But when we think of our own deepest being, our sense of who we really are, and where all reality is ultimately rooted, then the present moment, integrating our whole reality, becomes the revelation of the Eternal.

It is to help us realize this revelation that we are given the Sabbath and told to keep it holy. The Sabbath is the sacramental representative of God's eternity: it reveals it, and it enables one to enter into it. All the sacraments enable us to contact a reality that is always present, although the sacrament itself stands apart from everyday experience in order to call attention to itself and thereby to the reality that it mediates. The Sabbath is not really one time among other times, but the underlying eternity, which is, "all the time."

Thus the weekly celebration of the Sabbath — and much more the annual observance of the Great Sabbath — is the symbolic representation, the sacramental experience, of that aspect of our own reality that transcends time. Erich Fromm points out that human beings are like God in being gifted with "soul, with reason, love, freedom," and in these respects are "not subject to time or death." But insofar as we live through biological bodies in the context of cosmic nature, we are subject to time and death. Many ancient peoples offered sacrifices to the divinities of death and of time, hoping to appease them and hold off their voracious appetites for human flesh. The Bible, says Fromm, in its revelation of the Sabbath, takes a completely different approach. It goes to the root of the threat and "eliminates time" by stopping all work that interferes with nature. Where there is no attempt to move things out of their natural courses, to transform the environment by the exercise of human will — that is, to bring about change — there is (by definition, so to speak) no time. The symbolic meaning is that for that day, the Sabbath, time is suspended, and we live in eternity.[5] It reminds us that although in our temporal embodiment we are subject to change and dissolution, through our tie to God, to the Eternal One, we also live beyond time.

This knowledge that we are fundamentally victorious over time (see John 16:33) gives a sense of release and freedom, even while we continue to be faithful and persevering in our temporal responsibilities. The deepest part of our consciousness knows that we live in eternity, that sabbath consciousness is the underlying consciousness on which the six working days develop their finite and relative forms.

But the Sabbath is not a finite and relative form. It is, in Jewish piety, the image and the consort of the Invisible, the Formless God. The Sabbath, in Jewish sacred lore, is personified as the bride of God and queen. She is welcomed at sundown on Friday with the happy strains of the "Lekha Dodi," a song composed by a sixteenth-century member of the Safed group of Kabbalists and sung to this day in the synagogues:

> Beloved, come, the bride to meet,
> The Sabbath Princess let us greet.
> Arouse thyself, awake and shine,
> Thy light has come, the light divine;
> Awake and sing, and over thee
> The glory of the Lord shall be.
> Crown of thy husband, come in peace;
> Let joy and gladsome song increase
> Among his faithful, sorrow-tried,
> His chosen people — come, O bride.[6]

The union of God with his bride, the Sabbath — or, in another image, the Shekhina, the divine presence — is the Jewish mystic's way of pointing to the wholeness of the Absolute.[7] All the polarities of life are resolved into unity; whatever had been separated is reconciled.

Sabbath consciousness in us means the conjunction of opposites, the balancing and harmonization of our polarized qualities, the integration of our erstwhile fragmented selves, the realization of our profound unity. But this profound unity, in which we participate in the unity of God, must be a unity beyond form. Only the Infinite, the Formless, can ground all forms. Sabbath consciousness is formless, like the God to whom it is united. This is why it is characterized by the cessation of works, of change.

Thus the Sabbath, emblem of God's motionlessness, or rest, is reflected in our sabbath consciousness. It is not doing anything; it is not even being any particular kind of thing; it is just *being itself*. The works of motion and manifestation are withdrawn, called back into the abyss of the Godhead, into Invisibility, into This Day, into Paradise.

"Be with Me in Paradise"

"Be with Me in Paradise." We initially hear these words as a promise. How would we feel if we heard them as a plea — especially remembering the prayer, "Father, I desire that they be with me ... "? And then how would we feel if we heard them as invitation and empowerment? Are they parallel to the call to Peter from across the night sea, "Come!" (Matt. 19:29)? Perhaps we don't believe that we can actually be "in Paradise" as a stage in our spiritual life. Perhaps we are afraid to believe it. But the Jesus who walks on the water and calls to us to "Come!" also reassures us, "Take heart, it is I; have no fear." If he says of the little children, "Let them come to me; don't forbid them" (Matt. 19:14), and beckons and urges the rest of us, "Come to me, all of you ... " (Matt. 11:28), shall we not have confidence to go forward?

What does it mean for us to be in Paradise? "Paradise" is derived from a Persian word for an enclosed garden, planted with trees and flowers. It became for the Jews a term for the resting place of the dead awaiting resurrection. To whom does Jesus promise it? This man has been called "the Good Thief," perhaps because he "stole" Paradise, for he obtained it for the asking. It has also been suggested (without scholarly historical support) that he was a freedom fighter, someone involved in the struggle to liberate the Chosen People from the secular power, the power of the "world." He is further delineated as having discrimination and insight: he declares that Jesus "has done nothing wrong" and asks to be remembered in the kingdom.

All this, of course, is representative of us as we enter "Paradise." We know the difference between limited life and full life; we have built our aspirations and our preliminary efforts around the ideal of attaining freedom; and in the end we rely entirely on divine grace and believe in its promise and power. Divine grace means (among other things) being "remembered" by God: gathered together, member by member, reintegrated, at-one-ed, made "whole." To be in Paradise is to be at-one-with ourselves, all other beings, and God. And this answers to God's desire to be at-one-with us — God's desire, "Be with me." When God has us satisfactorily "with" Godself, then God is "remembering" us in the sense of carrying us in God's full and loving attention, enabling us to participate in the divine life, enabling us to see the glory given in love before the foundation of the world (John 17:24; cf. Col. 3:4). We are seeing it within God, because we are now thoroughly at-one-ed with God.

This is the significance of believing in the Incarnation: we believe, we are convinced, we see that we human beings can be and are One-Being-With God. It is this faith that enables us to enter Paradise. If we don't believe that we can be with God, in God, in Paradise, why then, of course, we can't. If we don't believe that our life can somehow be taken up and joined with God's life, then it can't. If we don't believe that we are given glory in God's love for us, then how can we see it? But Jesus shows it to us, urges us not to be afraid to believe rather than to doubt, and calls us, "Come!" "Be with me where I am!"

Bruno Barnhart says that this is Jesus' one great work, the manifestation of the new union of humanity with God, which is itself the Great Sabbath. This is the Sabbath intended for humanity (Mark 2:27), "in which the human person is freed to be with God, 'as in the beginning,' in the garden," in Paradise. The sacramental Sabbath, especially Holy Saturday, "is a ritual anticipation of this communion of God and humanity, to be realized once Jesus has made humanity 'equal with God'" (John 5:18).[8]

Now has come the fulfillment of what was pointed to in the parable of the talents: "Well done.... Enter into your master's joy" (Matt. 25:21). Doing is over and joy surrounds us. The capacity for joy is in all of us. There is, in fact, a bliss level of our spiritual reality that is structurally a central aspect of our very being. Jesus says that our "angels always behold the face of my Father" (Matt. 18:10). It may be that relations in the spiritual realm are so intimate and so borderless that our angels are not only exalted personal beings in their own right but also communicate their beatific vision to the highest and most inward aspect of our consciousness. More inward than the body or the breath of biological life, more central than the mind and memory, above even the intellectual intuition, is the indwelling bliss that is our innermost clothing. When we enter into our inner chamber, when we sink into the depths of our hearts, when we seek for the divine spirit in the center of our being, we come upon this hidden bliss.

This bliss is an absolute. It is not contrasted with an opposite; it has no opposite. You are in the Paradise of this bliss when the cross ceases to torment you, when the opposites no longer oppose each other, and you find yourself at their intersection. When no particular form is imposed on the affective consciousness, it settles into original beatitude. This is not an apathy that is certainly inferior to the world of pleasure and pain, but it is the spiritual realm of the God of Nothing, transcendent of all relative qualities, the Infinite above all finite experiences limited and defined by their comparisons with one another. Pleasure (and pain) is something that comes and goes. It is a "treasure on earth, where moth and rust consume and thieves break through and steal." This is not what we seek. Therefore we have to persist until we find the "treasure in heaven" which is not subject to these contingencies.

This treasure is in our heart (Matt. 6:19–21). It is abiding joy, and when we have entered into it, we will not be elated by success or depressed by failure, proud when praised and shamed when blamed. Such responses will become meaningless to us. Surrounded and permeated by the glory of God's own joy, how can we care for, even notice, such ways of valuing our life? How can we possibly be interested in receiving glory from other human beings on our small planet when we already have the uncreated "glory that comes from the One God" (John 5:44)?

What we feel in Paradise is the basic bliss of reality. It is the ground state of our sense of the goodness of existence, an ontological joy. Just as God is Unlimited Existence, while creatures are beings whose existence is limited to some particular form, so God's beatitude is unlimited, or form-less, delight. We experience pleasure or pain because of something, some relation of our sensibility to some stimulus. But absolute, transcendental bliss is not dependent on anything but existence itself and consciousness itself. It is the fundamental and unconditioned affectivity that rejoices in God's unconditioned being and love. It is always here: we ourselves are it. When we hold still enough, are silent enough, keep Sabbath enough, we become aware of it. Like the wind, it doesn't come from anywhere — it has no cause — and it doesn't go anywhere — it has no goals. It just is in perfect freedom. Everyone who is born of the Spirit is like that (John 3:8).

Exercises

1. When you first read this chapter, you can take several days in which to study it and to practice these exercises. If you are doing this over a weekend, one of these days will actually be a Sabbath (Friday evening through Saturday). I propose that we keep it in some traditional way, with glowing candles and happy family meals and with leisure and quiet in between. For beautiful ways to keep the Sabbath weekly, see Tilden Edwards, *Sabbath Time* (Nashville: Upper Room, 1992) and Marva J. Dawn, *Keeping the Sabbath Wholly: Ceasing, Resting, Embracing, Feasting* (Grand Rapids: Eerdmans, 1989). We have to resist a great deal in our minds and senses and consciences in order to do this. Our culture urges us to keep busy. The conscience formed in this work-achievement culture can always find something that we "ought" to be doing. I suggest that you plan and arrange your life in such a way that you can have some hours on Saturday when you do not "have to" do anything.

2. Don't use all this time to rush to some other activity, even something as fine as painting or music or reading. Spend a significant portion of it doing *nothing*. Do it outdoors, if possible. *Be,* in the natural scene. Feel the weather, walk on the earth, sit on it, look at the sky, the trees, the flowers, the river, the sea, the mountains, the far horizon, the rocks, the animals. Be with them

all. In silence. In contentment. Listen to the quiet, if you can be where it is quiet. At least listen to the quiet in your own mind.

3. And that's the point. Let the mind fall silent, let it be still for a while. Don't try to do anything; don't even "try to" keep your mind silent. Remember that *God's* Sabbath is being kept in you, and that is all that matters. Rest in that.

4. After a while, you will notice three things: (*a*) a sense of deep satisfaction, contentment. It does not undertake to justify itself, to say why it is there, to give a rational account of itself. It is just there, unmistakably there. (*b*) Following on this, you will find an upsurge of confidence, a bright warm vital feeling of sureness and competence. This is the *pistis* ("faith") that Jesus said would be the power of our new life. It is a curious feeling, for it is an awareness of the power-presence of God as our own life. This strong, clear, sure energy is God's, but it appears in me as my own confidence and capability. (*c*) When this has surfaced, it overflows. We begin to feel how God's "virtue," i.e., *potency,* radiates from us. In a way, we have nothing to do with it. It just happens in and through us. But it is also true that we are completely involved in this outflow, totally willing it, ourselves. With all our heart. All my life has become letting God happen through me.

5. This is the answer to God's prayer, "Be with me." Keep this sense with you when your quiet time stirs itself into active time. Remember that this is the truth. You have a right to be happy in it, and you can be happy in it, no matter what your circumstances, because it is unconditional happiness, absolute happiness. God is happy *in you.*

6. On Holy Saturday go to your church or your favorite prayer place in the daytime, perhaps around the middle of the day. Reread this chapter. Then just open yourself to the Silence, the Nothingness, the Reality, the Oneness, the Joy. Stay as long as you like. In the late afternoon make a last review of your Lent and preparation for the renewal of your Baptism.

— *Nine* —

BAPTISMAL TRANSFORMATION

ࢠ

WHEN THE SUN has set on the Great Sabbath, the Vigil of the Resurrection begins. In the ancient church it may have gone on all night. The catechumens had been preparing for this throughout Lent with lessons every day and examinations at intervals. Various sacramental ceremonies may have taken place along the way: exorcisms of evil spirits, anointing of breast and back with healing oil, symbolic purification of hearing and speaking (openness to the Word), tasting the salt of Wisdom. During this final night they may have heard the entire Gospel of Mark or of John read to them, interspersed perhaps with psalms and hymns and prayers, until at dawn they were baptized (by immersion) and came up out of the water to face the rising sun.

The mysteries are now reaching their highest pitch. Several revelations remain to be made. We are still in the middle day of the holy Triduum: the first day (Good Friday) effecting our *separation* from the forms of the world, the second day (Holy Saturday) conducting us through the *initiation* proper, and the third day (Easter Sunday) leading us forth into the *return* to the world. The whole constitutes our baptismal transformation, of which the Baptism with water sacramentally marks the "turning" point, the conversion.

Conversion and Redemption

From the way Holy Saturday was described, it may have seemed that we had come to the end of our story. But this is not so. We may have thought that we had to be "converted" in order to be eligible for Paradise, but I am going to suggest that it's just the other way around: we have to experience Paradise before we can be thoroughly converted. I believe that many things are turned around, inverted, reversed at this point. "The first shall be last, and the last shall be first." What we thought was the first step may turn out to be the last step, and indeed what we may have thought would be the last step may reveal itself as the first step in a new world and a new life.

The real initiation takes place after the death of the Word, after outward — organism-serving — concepts and words are abandoned as no longer the focus of interest. In the Lesser Mysteries we thought that death was the end, but in the Greater, we find that it is the beginning. All that went before was only preliminary. Now we are lifted into the supernatural life. Perhaps this is what the ranks of the angels symbolize: the grades of consciousness developed beyond the conative/concept/word level. A tantalizing glimpse of what this may have meant in the first century or two of Christian life can be caught in a letter of Ignatius, bishop of Antioch and disciple of St. John:

> Might I not write to you things more full of mystery? But I fear to do so, lest I should inflict injury on you who are but babes. Pardon me in this respect, lest, as not being able to receive their weighty import, you should be strangled by them. For even I, though I am bound (for Christ) and am able to understand heavenly things, the angelic orders, and the different sorts of angels and hosts, the distinction between powers and dominions, and the diversities between thrones and authorities, the mightiness of the aeons, and the preeminence of the cherubim and seraphim, the sublimity of the Spirit, the kingdom of the Lord, and above

all the incomparable majesty of Almighty God — though
I am acquainted with these things, yet am I not therefore
by any means perfect, nor am I such a disciple as Paul or
Peter....For I now begin to be a disciple...initiated into
the mysteries of the Gospel.[1]

What these meanings were was evidently included in the secret
teaching of which the early Fathers write. This teaching was
transmitted only orally, explains Clement of Alexandria, who
presided over an important catechetical school around 200 C.E.:

Secret things are entrusted to speech, not writing....This
is certainly so in the case of what has to do with God...
[lest unprepared readers] should stumble by taking [these
teachings] in a wrong sense; and...we should be found
"reaching a sword to a child"...[However] the Saviour
has taught the Apostles...[and] the unwritten rendering
of the written has been handed down also to us...[who,
with the power of the Holy Spirit, will eventually] become
able to look the splendors of truth in the face.[2]

This vision of "the splendors of truth" is referred to by Clement's pupil Origen, who says that Jesus showed himself to be
very different in his real appearance when on the "Mountain"
(Mt. Tabor, the Transfiguration) from what those saw who
could not "follow him so high."[3] Peter, James, and John were
the sole witnesses to this "splendor," and, intimate disciples
though they were, even they found it overwhelming.

Those who cannot climb so high yet, says Origen, see in the
Gospel only stories that they take to be historical narratives,
with at most perhaps moral or faith-related teachings attached,
but the intention of the Gospel writer was "to convey a secret
meaning in the garb of history, that those who have the capacity
may work out for themselves all that related to the subject."[4]

The Scriptures were written by the Spirit of God, and have
a meaning, not only such as is apparent at first sight, but
also another, which escapes the notice of most. For those

[words] which are written are the forms of certain mysteries, and the images of divine things...not known to all, but to those only on whom the grace of the Holy Spirit is bestowed.[5]

This grace of the Holy Spirit, or the initiation into "the mysteries of Jesus," is offered "only to the holy and the pure...whose soul has, for a long time, been conscious of no evil....Let such a one hear the doctrines which were spoken in private by Jesus to his genuine disciples." It seems that these words were part of the opening speech of the celebrant of the ceremony of the "initiating of those who were already purified into the Sacred Mysteries."[6]

These fragments of ancient history show us that in the early days "conversion" meant a great deal more than forsaking a sinful life or adopting a belief system. It meant a kind of metamorphosis, really, a change of one's whole form of being, that comes about from the revelation that appears in Christ. These "mysteries" are spoken of at several places in the New Testament, but one of the most memorable passages is in Paul's Epistle to the Colossians:

> I became [the church's] servant...to make the word of God fully known, the mystery, [that which] having been hidden [*apokekrymmenon*: cf. "cryptography," writing in a secret code] from the [indefinite or infinite] ages [the aeons, the rank of angels mentioned above, who are immortal] and from the generations [people, who are mortal and preserve their lines by reproduction, or generation] but now manifested to his saints, to whom God wished to make known among the nations what is the riches of the glory of this mystery, which is *Christ in you*. (Col. 1:26–27)

We ourselves are still "babes" in these matters, but we do perhaps know correctly a few things. The sacrament of Baptism portends a radical and tremendous change in our mode of life, likened to birth: the whole context changes, our point of view changes, our sense of identity, our way of interrelating, our appreciation of meanings and values. What we had thought we were and what was important for us is swept away, and a completely new revelation of what we are and what is important for us takes its place.

We may also feel safe in seeing that the sacrament of the Eucharist, by making food, the eating of food — which food is the living Body of the incarnate God — its central symbol, reveals that this new life involves a most profound intimacy and union with the God who incarnates, an intimacy and union that is productive of life, further life, growing life, abundant life. The union takes place on all levels of Being — his and ours (which he shares) — the body, its life (blood), the human soul, and the divinity: body to body, life to life, soul to soul, divinity to divinity. An important corollary, I believe, is that this union establishes and reveals that the life is both eternal and growing. This which we receive and pass on by "generation" and that which is by nature "immortal and eternal in the heavens" exchange and share their characteristics. We find that the first has become last by incarnation, and the last has become first by grace of elevation.

This "conversion" by which the divine becomes "converted into" the human experience and the human is "converted into" the divine experience now shows in the depth psychology of the human being, as the imprisoned powers are "redeemed" and set free. The Apostles' Creed says that Jesus "descended into hell," and the First Letter of Peter says that he "went and preached to the spirits in prison, who formerly did not obey" (1 Pet. 3:19–20). I am going to interpret this as something that actually happens in our own depths and constitutes our "conversion" and "redemption" proper.

Let us go back to the Paradise experience, for this is where the conversion, the turning around, actually starts. "Paradise," we remember, means the great bliss of being at the Heart, being consciously in God, being at the foundation and core of all Being, Unity, Truth, Goodness, and Beauty, being one's real self, being enlightened, being free. It also means the liberating joy of realizing the divine unconditional love. This makes us feel totally secure and completely fulfilled. Now, it is this deep satisfaction of the Paradise experience that makes possible what happens next.

When we are deeply centered, when we have tasted the bliss of Paradise, when we are thoroughly reassured and thus "relieved" (Matt. 11:28: *anapausō*), then a great transformation occurs in our depths where there is a "prison" holding our "spirits who formerly did not obey." Think of St. Paul confessing — and complaining — that the things he wants to do he does not do, and what he resolves he will not do, that is the very thing he finds himself doing. But all actions begin as consciousness-movements in the mind/heart. Trying to control these by sheer will-power, as St. Paul testifies, does not work. Issuing commandments to control your behavior, reinforced by sanctions, promises of rewards and threats of punishments, is not the way to achieve transformation. You have to go down to the root and relieve whatever is wrong there. This is why Jesus is represented as going down into hell to set the prisoners free.

And he does it by preaching Good News — neither threats nor rewards, but truth. When you can know that truth, it will set you free (1 Pet. 4:6; John 8:32). The Good News, of course, is the truth of God's unconditional love for us and the divine intimacy with the human, assuring us of our own immortality and the release of the goodness that is in us.

The spirits in prison are the consciousness-energies in us, our spiritual powers shackled by fear and pain and therefore unable to move in accord with the true generosity of the real self. They are aspects of ourselves — not only individually but collectively, culturally, as a race — that have been so hurt by experience in the world that they have devoted themselves entirely to self-protection: withdrawal, heavy armor, ready offensive action, accumulation of goods for oneself, including power and honor — whatever we think will secure satisfactory being for us. But, of course, none of these efforts quite brings it off. Our powers remain inhibited, imprisoned, unable to express their natural expansiveness. Meanwhile, we are living in "hypocrisy" by not being our real self. We are always living as pretend-selves and always hating it. Jesus rightly identified hypocrisy as the fundamental trouble and set to work to turn it around by making it possible for us to know and to accept the full truth about ourselves.

Before our conversion, we are like a field grown with both wheat and tares. Tares are a kind of weed that wraps its root around the root of the wheat, so that you can't pull up the weed without uprooting the good plant as well. Some myths of the spiritual journey describe the discovery of both demons and benevolent deities in the secret places of the soul.[7] When we see the failings in ourselves, we feel horror and despondency. Yet there are also amazing powers for compassion, self-sacrifice, insights into truth, aspirations toward the Good, love for God and neighbor; there are places of tranquillity and peace and faith; and there are great reserves of energy. These are all mixed together in our subterranean consciousness, whence they influence our feelings and behaviors. We are somewhat conscious of them and become more so as we practice and progress in the spiritual life. But until we *know* that we are safe without our own efforts at self-protection, we cannot totally release them: the "demons" as unnecessary and the "angels" as free to operate fully.

My suggestion is that it is only when these imprisoned powers hear the Good News — the truth of God's love and of their own belonging to divine life — that the bonds fall away. All those investments in protection drop off, are no longer relevant. All our guilts and fears and hatreds and griefs and refusals to love, our memories of hurt, our repressed feelings, whatever we have in our hell-prison, the Christ-Spirit heals and releases. And what makes us relax and open up enough for this to happen is our taste of the Paradise experience. I think at least some of that has to come first. This is a reversal of what we have usually been taught, perhaps. We aren't required to produce all the correct feelings and behaviors first, and then God will give us heaven.

First God gives us (at least a taste of) heaven, so that we can feel secure enough to let go and let our own real goodness (which we have to have, being created by God) come out (1 John 4:10, 19; Rom. 5:8).

The feeling that we have when this truth really penetrates our consciousness is quite truly called "redemption." It feels like being let out of prison, like being released from slavery. This was probably the primary image in the ancient world, in which the biggest change in life imaginable was that from the state of enslavement to freedom.[8] This is also the image shown us in the Easter Vigil readings, which include the escape of the children of Israel from the slave camps of Egypt. The great Exodus to the Promised Land tells with mythic power of the spiritual journey and the love and faithfulness of God. Later, the return from the Babylonian Captivity repeats the theme. These stories resonate with us because they have very sensitive analogs in our interior lives.

Having released by his message of Good News the imprisoned "spirits who formerly did not obey," Christ brings these liberated captives back in his "Triumph," his parade into the city after achieving a great conquest. In the Epistle to the Ephesians, St. Paul says: "Therefore it is said, 'When he ascended on high he led a host of captives, and he gave gifts to men.' (In saying, 'He ascended,' what does it mean but that he had also descended into the lower parts of the earth? He who descended is he who also ascended far above all the heavens, that he might fill all things)" (Eph. 4:8–10). The psalm that Paul is quoting here is Psalm 68, and it says, "You have gone up on high and led captivity captive; you have received gifts even from your enemies." This is the point for us. Even those consciousness movements that had been contrary to our spiritual aspirations are now converted. They are turned around and all their energies directed toward the divine life. Those powers in us have given their strength now to the Christ life; even the erstwhile enemies have contributed their gifts.

This is why the second day of the holy Triduum follows the

first day (in this interpretation). It is because it is the freeing power of Paradise that unlocks the gates of hell. When Peter saw and confessed the divine power and love resident in the humanity of Jesus — that is, *present to* humanity, for the *sake of* humanity — Jesus exclaimed that the whole life that he was trying to establish and build up would be based on this insight, and "the gates of hell would not prevail against" its power to crush them (Matt. 16:18). The great relief we experience in the bliss of heaven makes it possible for us to let go of the cramping, repressive restraints we had put on our prisoners. Because of the light and warmth of the divine unconditional love, these buried energies now have no need to protect or avenge themselves, to grieve or to hate, to run away or to strike. The foundation of pain and sin has been taken away. This is what happens in the Great Sabbath and why it transforms and releases all the energies of consciousness. All that spiritual power that had been pent up is now available for life. St. Peter says, "This is why the gospel [is] preached even to the dead, ... so that they might live in the spirit like God" (1 Pet. 4:6).

Enlightenment

One of the images for conversion is the passage from death to life. Thus the First Epistle of John says, "We know that we have passed out of death into life, because we love the brethren" (1 John 3:14). We can now understand this in two ways. One is the more usual meaning, that we human beings love one another, which we are now free to do because the ground for suspicion, protection, hatred, envy, and all the other forces that prevented love has now been dissolved by the realization of God's love for us and for all and by the insight into our own participation in divine life. The second meaning is interior and follows from the interpretation of the descent into hell offered above. There is now love among our interior "brethren," the various energies of our deep self. There is congenial affinity among them; they can live together organically. We are free of internal contradiction and strife. And this, of course, greatly facilitates the unconditional (free) love of other persons. It is only with a true self of our own that we can truly love the selves of others.

This theme can also be developed in terms of a second image for conversion and redemption, the passage from darkness to light. In the early church Baptism was sometimes called "Enlightenment," *phōtismos* in Greek. We have some hint of this in Ephesians 5:14, where St. Paul quotes what was evidently already a well-known liturgical utterance: "Awake, sleeper, and rise from the dead, and Christ shall give you light." Perhaps our own custom of giving the newly baptized a lighted candle can be traced to this ancient way of celebrating the mystery. In that same passage, St. Paul speaks in terms of this metaphor, saying, "You once were darkness, but now you are light in the Lord; walk as children of light (for the fruit of light is found in all that is good and right and true)" (Eph. 5:8–9). The enlightened self, awakened from the dead, is the true self, right, and good, and it is able to be that way because it has passed through the Paradise experience of the Sabbath. Hebrews 6 speaks of those who have been "enlightened, who have tasted the heavenly gift, and have become partakers of the Holy Spirit, and have savored the goodness of the word of God and the powers of the age to come" (Heb. 6:4–5).

This is conversion, turning around, in this sense: All through the first part of the spiritual life we were striving toward God and toward the true self in the heart of our being. We had to strip off everything that was relative, limited, referenced to the particular self that identified itself by its negation of other selves. When this self, with all its categories of understanding and attempts to grasp God by words and concepts, was thoroughly "dead," then we found ourselves in the bliss of the divine life itself, unlimited being, meaning, value, love, beauty. At this point we are able to "turn around" in the sense of facing the other way. United with God, we now face outward, as if moving into manifestation *from* God *toward* the world. This is the original creative movement, the path (Way) of the Word itself. Being born of the Holy Spirit, filled with God's living breath, we are blown into manifestation, we are "spoken." This begins with our most interior manifestation, those deep energies, no longer prisoners or slaves, but followers of the Word, and united brethren among themselves. These energies we may suppose are "the powers of the age to come." At least, they are the first movement, which will empower further movements, of the new life into which we now enter. We had been in darkness, looking toward the light. Now we ourselves "are light in the Lord," and are starting to shine into the darkness. "The light shines in the darkness, and the darkness can no longer hold it down" (John 1:5).

The powers of darkness had in the past controlled many aspects of our lives. For instance, most human societies have decided that internalized aversive experiences are the most effective way of controlling social behavior. So they have taught their children to feel shame and guilt. These feelings are so unpleasant that most people will exert themselves a good deal to avoid them. They are excellent motivators.

But the Gospel message of Jesus — the Good News — is that all that is unnecessary. You are not to feel shame or guilt anymore. Of course, you are not to behave immorally anymore, either. But, then, you won't have any motive to do so, because you will know yourself to be totally loved and absolutely secure. "No one born of God commits sin; for he cannot sin, because he is born of God" (1 John 3:9).

The only catch is that you will not be *physically* secure in this life. You will know yourself to be *absolutely* secure as a person — secure in your immortal, eternal life, and secure in being completely loved. But in this world you may meet with all sorts of misfortune. The Epistle to the Hebrews points out that even "after you were enlightened, you endured a hard struggle with sufferings, sometimes being publicly exposed to abuse and affliction, and sometimes being partners with those so treated.

For you had compassion on the prisoners, and you joyfully accepted the plundering of your property, since you knew that you yourselves had a better possession and an abiding one" (Heb. 10:32–34).

The key is: Do not identify with the aspects of your apparent self that are suffering the misfortunes. If your body suffers an accident, illness, or deprivation, remember that you are not the body; you are life itself (Sermon on the Mount, Matt. 6:25). If your personality, your psychological or emotional life, suffers distress from injustice or rejection, remember that your true self exists under the protection of God, and although all these things should befall you, "not a hair of your head shall fall" (Luke 21:18). And most important, when you are tempted to reject yourself and to feel shame and chagrin and despair because your behaviors, thoughts, or feelings do not live up to your ideal standards, remember that you are loved by God and by the heavenly community *unconditionally*. "Therefore do not throw away your confidence, . . . so that you may do the will of God and receive what is promised" (Heb. 10:35–36).

This is the Good News. It begins as promises. But as we grow and pass through the mystery of Baptism, the promises turn into insight. We see for ourselves, directly, that these things are true. The more we see them and know them to be true, the more we lose our fear of existence. As we lose our fear of existence, we loosen our grasping hold on it, our fierce concern to protect ourselves and to destroy whatever might injure us. We begin to see that *we cannot be injured*. Therefore there is no need to defend anything. We are quite safe. This is "salvation."

This salvation, or knowledge of being safe, comes from God's love for us, directly and indirectly: directly, as loving us as persons unconditionally, and indirectly, as having created us as indestructible persons, whose true being cannot suffer injury.

The Easter mystery is about the death of the "darkness" way of experiencing ourselves and the coming to life of the "enlightened" way of experiencing ourselves. Identification with a self that needs protection and that motivates us to try to secure ourselves, injuring others in the process, perishes in the face of the realization that this is not what we are or what we need to do in order to live abundantly. As this falsehood dies, there rises up in us the sure knowledge that we are beloved children of God, heirs of eternal life, and the world turns completely around.

How long does it take to undergo this Baptism? Probably time has very little to do with it. It seems usually to be a long, gradual process in most of us. But it can be sudden. The scales can fall from your eyes and you can see that you had it all backward (Acts 9:18), that your situation is almost the exact opposite of what you had thought. Instead of being fragile, threatened, unloved, unlovable, and forsaken by God as an unworthy sinner, you are actually the beloved child of God, completely secure in eternal life, in whom God finds delight (Matt. 3:17). This is "the true light that enlightens everyone" (John 1:9): that "God gave us eternal life" (1 John 5:11) and that we have this testimony in ourselves (1 John 5:10).

With this realization all inclination to what we call sin or evil disappears: "anyone born of God does not sin" (1 John 5:18). There is no motive for it. We are already as safe and as rich and as happy as we can be. When we have realized this, we become "the light of the world," capable of giving light in our turn. It is this light *that we are* that we are to "let shine" (Matt. 5:14–16), and we now do so. All our energy radiates out — as it is its nature to do; we don't have to force it or push it — in love for others. We would have been doing this before now, except that we were so preoccupied with our own hurts and fears. But now we have no fear, for "there is no fear in love, but perfect love [God's love for us] casts out [our] fear" (1 John 4:18).

Unification in "The Only One"

Early Syrian Christianity sees Baptism under yet another image, *unification,* or re-integration. The central thought is that now humanity is restored ("redeemed") to its original unity and purity and fullness of being. No longer enslaved or suppressed or divided or scattered, it is its own true self. This is very much related to the radical negative work that led up to the Great Sabbath, because the divisive descriptions and comparative values are what had to be stripped away and forgotten in order to reveal the true oneness: of the person, of the person with God, of all persons in God and with one another.

The Gospel of Thomas, which may have been originally written in Syriac and later translated into the Coptic in which we have recently recovered it, stresses this teaching. And here we see further instances of the reversals and inversions that typify "conversion." Logion 4 in Thomas says the elderly shall consult the newborn and learn wisdom from them, for "many who are first shall be last and they shall become *a single one*." Another text says:

> Jesus said to them, "When you make the two *one,* and when you make the inner as the outer and the outer as the inner and the above as the below, and when you make the male and the female into a *single one,* so that the male will not be male and the female not be female,... then shall you enter the kingdom." (Logion 22)

As this verse strives to clarify, it is not so much a complementarity that is expected as it is a *transcendence* of the very possibility of that sort of polarity. Probably other examples would be the rich and the poor, or the lords and servants whose ranks were dismissed at the Last Supper to be replaced by coequal "friends." Friends and enemies would be a further figure, and so would the value polarities mentioned in the Beatitudes, where those who are usually accounted unfortunate are acclaimed as supremely happy.

All these figures can be seen as pointing to the original unity of the moment of creation, when all humanity was simply "Adam," the living soul made of the earth but in the image and likeness of God.[9] This is why the transcendence of the sexual duality is especially mentioned; it indicates the "time" (state) before the original Adam was divided. Baptism is understood to effect a return to this condition. This is stated by St. Paul:

> For as many of you as were baptized into Christ have put on Christ. There is neither Jew nor Greek, there is neither slave nor free, there is neither male nor female; for you are all one in Christ Jesus. (Gal. 3:27–28)

> By one Spirit we were all baptized into one body — Jews or Greeks, slaves or free.... (1 Cor. 12:13)

> Here there cannot be Greek and Jew, circumcised and uncircumcised, barbarian, Scythian, slave, free man, but Christ is all, and in all. (Col. 3:11)

The point being made is not merely that we are no longer to order ourselves socially in terms of these classes, but that we are to experience ourselves in our original unity transcending any comparative description whatsoever. The early Syrian ascetical writer Aphrahat stresses this by saying, "There is no such thing as male and female"[10] or slave/free, or Jew/Greek, or friend/enemy, and so on. And the reason for this is that Baptism has made us all one in Christ, "The Only One."

Robert Murray tells us that the Syriac word *iḥidaya* is the equivalent of the Greek *monogenēs,* which figures so prominently in John 1:18. God is by nature invisible, but the *Monogenēs* God, reposing in the Emptiness of the Invisible One, reveals the sacred mysteries. *Monogenēs* is usually translated "only-begotten." Perhaps we can also read "singly generated," "unitively generated," or "generated as Only One." "Only One" is what *iḥidaya* means. For the Syrians, Baptism meant wholeness in oneself, not needing another to be one's completion in the flesh; single-mindedness, devoted entirely to the new life of God in Christ; and being joined and unified with Christ, the Only One.[11] Aphrahat expresses this by saying that "Jesus, the Only One [*iḥidaya*], who is from the bosom of the Father, shall cause 'those who are one' [*iḥidaye*] to rejoice."[12]

Back of this there seems to be not only the Jewish sense of the One God, but the Greek sense of the priority of the One over the Many. Thomas Logion 75 says, "Jesus said, 'Many are standing at the door, but the solitary (unitary) are the ones who will enter the bridal chamber.'" A Syriac Epiphany hymn declares, "Whoever is baptized and puts on the Only One, the Lord of the many, occupies the place of the many, for Christ becomes his great Treasure."[13] In the famous response to Martha's complaint about Mary's not helping her, there is the suggestion that "the many" are associated with anxiety and trouble, while "the one" is associated with the Necessary, which is further declared to be the Good (Luke 10:40). In Matthew 6:22, there is a stern directive to have a "single" eye; the Greek word is *haplous*, meaning "onefold, single, all in one way, not compound or double, absolute." And this state is identified with enlightenment.

I am inclined to think that this injunction against "doubling" the mind — which seems to be what the New Testament means by "doubting" — gives a good clue to the deep significance of the opposite of "doubting," namely, "believing" or having "faith."[14] "Faith" is frequently said to be what makes "wholeness."[15] Indeed, all potentialities seem to be rooted in this spiritual state of wholeness-faith-unity: "All things are possible to the one believing" (Mark 9:23). A very interesting passage is Mark 11:22–24:

> Jesus says: "Have the faith of God. Truly I tell you that whoever says to this mountain, 'Be taken up and cast into the sea,' and does not doubt in his heart, but believes that what he says happens, it will be to him [=he will have it]. Therefore, I tell you, all things which you pray and ask, believe that you received, and it will be to you."

The word for "doubt" is *diakrithē*, which means to "divide, separate." "Heart" is the core of one's being. "The faith of God" seems a curious expression, for we are more used to hearing of "faith in God." But if "faith" means this absolute unity of the single mind, perhaps we are urged to be One as God is One. Consider Matthew 5:48: "You, therefore, be perfect as your heavenly Father is perfect." "Perfect" is *teleios,* with the connotation of "complete," agreeable to "whole" and "one." Absoluteness seems to be indicated, too, for the proof of the Father's perfection is his sending sun and rain indiscriminately (not doubling) on the good and the evil, thus transcending that polarity. Now look at John 17:22–23:

> "The glory which you have given me I have given to them, that they may be *one* even as we are *one,* I in them and you in me, that they having been *perfected in one,* the world may know that you did send me and did love them even as you did love me."

It all comes together here, the perfection, the unity, the love, and the glory. Gertrude Winkler quotes Thomas Logion 17, "I will give you...what has not arisen in the heart of man" and explains that this "is nothing less than the reality of becoming transformed into God's own glory."

> In Syria this transformation often is described in biblical language; to be robed in glory is to put on Christ....This New Testament theme of "oneness," of becoming one by putting on the "One," very likely also lies behind the Syrian idea of Christ being the *iḥidaya,* the "Only One," whom the *iḥidaye,* "those who are one," put on at Baptism.[16]

This glory in unity, in the Only One, we may believe was the secret thing that could not be written down, or at least could not be set forth plainly, but had to be hidden under parables and similes and hinted at in apparently historical stories. But this must be the full meaning of the sacrament, the mystery of Baptism. It is the great revelation, the great change, conversion, the great liberation and release into the very freedom that is God.

When we participate in the Easter Vigil, witness the Baptism of the catechumens, and renew our own baptismal vows, we can be mindful of all that this means, of all that is implied, promised, revealed, and attested. All our efforts, all our surrender, all our dissolution, will at length have made us able, as Clement of Alexandria said, "to look the splendors of truth in the face."

Exercises

Like the last chapter, this one may be read more than once. The whole of your Lenten practice has been preparation for the renewal of your Baptism. This chapter focuses on that event. You will need two or three days to absorb it, and then you may want to review it — and your responses to these exercises — just before the Easter climax.

1. Meditate again on Paradise. Feel the security, the relief, the happiness of being with Jesus in Paradise *this day*.

2. Then experience in yourself how he sets the prisoners free. Whatever inhibited powers are enchained in you by fear, guilt, anger, or grief, let the Christ-power in you release them. Let them come forth, bearing their gifts in his triumph. Feel the "conversion" in yourself as these energies enter in proportioned ways into the integrality of a wholesome life.

3. Repeat these meditations in the days preceding Easter and again during Easter Season (and thereafter whenever they would be valuable).

4. Now turn attention to the renewal of baptismal vows in the Easter Vigil. (If this is not formally done in your church, you can still do the meditation by yourself.) Baptism replicates birth. The pool is the womb; the person is "born of God." Birth is when Breath (Spirit) first enters into you and you begin to live in a totally new, *much* larger and more complex world. Birth is a time of promise. There is so much potentiality in the new life. We make promises at our Baptism. Or is

it not more correct to say that God promises us and promises in us? In some congregations the baptized respond to the questions posed them by answering, "I will, with God's help." As you reread the baptismal service of your particular church and relive the commitment of your own Baptism, consider it in this light. These baptismal vows are mutual: I am promising God, but even more God is promising me. Meditate on this and feel confidence in it, instead of feeling anxiety about "living up to" what the promises require. Baptism with water takes a few seconds. Baptism with the Holy Spirit may well take a lifetime. We renew our Baptism every year for just this reason. We keep deepening it.

5. How do you want and intend to deepen your Baptism this year? In the context of this chapter, this means: with the sense of union with God that you now have, how can you strengthen and stabilize this, and poised there, in the heart of God, how can you do the works of God in the world?

6. To some extent we know what the truth about us is, and to some extent "it has not yet appeared what we shall be." Bruno Barnhart says, "Within each baptized person there dwells a new *beginning* which is to be drawn from again and again throughout life."[17] Seek the sense of "the beginning" in yourself. Feel its freedom, freshness, creative potential. It is new every year, the Easter celebration says. It is new every day. It is new every hour, every minute. God, by baptizing you, promises you that fresh Beginning over and over again, for correction if necessary, for further growth and delight always. Feel the confidence of that, the power of it, the joy of it.

7. We have been practicing Baptism for individuals. But notice that the Easter Vigil ritual calls for the whole congregation to renew baptismal vows and to be sprinkled with the newly made again baptismal water. Is this not a strong suggestion that the same kind of transformation needs to take place in communities *as communities,* that is, in terms of their *corporate* life? The fact that this rite is repeated every year indicates a recognition that the transformation is gradual but the demand for it

is relentless. How can my church, my congregation, deepen its baptismal realization? We might think also of the metaphor of Blood, which represents Life-Force, Energy, unconditional love. It isn't so much that the Blood is poured *out* of the body as that it is poured *into* the Body, living and circulating.

— Ten —

THE RESURRECTION
OF THE BODY

⌘

THUS WE COME to the third day of the sacred Triduum, the day of rising again. This has two meanings. The first is rising again to "where we were before" (cf. John 6:62). The second is the resurrection of the body. It is the first that makes the second possible.

Resurrection Fulfills Incarnation

There is a sense in which the whole of Jesus' earthly life was a "hidden life." His real nature isn't perfectly revealed until the resurrection. And even then it is a question of who can see it (John 14:19). But what it reveals is *what has always been,* the full truth about him. And so it is with us. We are the Spirit incarnated; we are trying to arrange that the Spirit should shine through the matter without impediment, so that the union of mortal and immortal is fully achieved.

Bringing these two things together — the mortal and the immortal, the earthly and the heavenly, the finite and the Infinite — is the central mystery of this mystery religion that we call Christianity. It's about "anointing" the world to be the real presence of God. This is what is celebrated in the Easter Vigil and

Eucharistic Feast. What we call "resurrection" is the full manifestation of the Incarnation itself. This is the revelation of what
and who we really are.

"Resurrection" means to be raised again, to go back up. This
follows from what was revealed to Nicodemus: that that which
rises to heaven is that which originally came down from heaven
(John 3:13).[1] It rises up again to that full, free, and blissful consciousness characteristic of all those who are born of the Spirit,
without origin or destination, beginning or end (John 3:8). It is
worth pointing out that resurrection in this (first) sense is identi-
cal with dying. We usually think of dying as the cessation of life
in the body and of resurrection as the return of life in the body.
But for someone who has come down from heaven to be "raised
again" means to return to heaven, and this is done by shedding
the body. In our interior sense, it is ceasing to identify with the
limitations of our ego-self. This is the so-called "death to self,"
and it is in itself the rising again to the true self, the heavenly
self. This is what I am calling the first sense of resurrection. It
is the central mystery event, but not the last one; it enables us
to see and to participate in the Incarnation, which will be developed in what I am calling the second sense of resurrection.
Taken together, resurrection and Incarnation reveal the whole
structure of reality and the value-laden movement of the world,
the "purpose" of life.

The divine Word "comes from the Source and comes into
the world; again, [it] leaves the world and goes back into the
Source" (John 16:28). It becomes incarnate as the world with
the intention of rising again and raising up all that has been
given it (John 6:38–39) — that is (in the interpretation I am of-
fering), with the intention of developing consciousness to the
point where it can be fully aware of its divine parentage. Our
mortality is to put on immortality (1 Cor. 15:53).

And the sign of this awareness is the sense of freedom, of
being released from some bondage or prison, which is why it
is also called "redemption." When some breakthrough occurs
for you, and you see something, and ripples of understanding

spread out on all sides with great waves of relief and joy, then you know that you have touched some kind and degree of truth. When you know the truth, it always sets you free (John 8:32). And when you experience this freedom, it is a confirmation to you that you have known the truth.

This is resurrection, this is rising again to where you were before. And it increases your capacity for significant incarnation. St. Paul says, "It is sown a physical body, it is raised a spiritual body. Thus it is written, 'The first humanity, Adam, was made a living being'; the ultimate humanity is to be a life-giving spirit" (1 Cor. 15:45). The ultimate humanity, the goal of the Incarnation, is to be a life-giving spirit.

But a life-giving spirit is divinity. It is God who gives life. To be God is to "have life in yourself" and therefore be able to give it to others, that is, to give them the power to "have life in themselves" and therefore the power to pass it on to still others. Life is always the power to give life. (That's why infertility has been felt as a curse.) So to be/become children of God is to have life in ourselves and the power to transmit it, to enable others to have life in themselves and to transmit it in their turn (John 5:26; 1:12).

Thus the divine life comes down from heaven and is sown in a perishable body. But the divine life gradually *rises up* as the imperishable that it truly is. The world itself is to be wrapped in the mantle of divine praise, the presence of the life-giving Spirit. And this takes place through us, the highly conscious elements of the world, the humanity made from "humus," from the dust of the earth, the dust of the stars, and organized into a "living being," which is ultimately to realize itself as the "life-giving Spirit."

> The first humanity was from the earth, a humanity of dust; the second humanity is from heaven.... Just as we have borne the image of the humanity of dust, we shall also bear the image of the humanity of heaven. (1 Cor. 15:47, 49)

We are the Mediator, the bread that comes down from heaven and gives life to the world: our flesh, our incarnation, for the life of the world (John 6:50–51).

Not only does our realization of divinity rise again, but our capacity for free incarnation, for being willingly "clothed with" the world, now emerges (2 Cor. 5:4). Sacrifices and offerings are no longer part of our religion; "but a body you have prepared for me...to do your will, O God" (Heb. 10:5). For we do not consider being equal to God something to be clung to, but we empty ourselves and take on the form of workers in the world, so that we become life-giving spirits (Phil. 2:6–7). We are constantly, day by day, coming down from heaven to become incarnate, clothed with the world, and constantly rising up again (John 13:3) to divine consciousness, our mortality and perishability having been re-clothed in the immortal and imperishable, whence we are willing and able to be "further clothed" in the world, in order to give it life, that God's will may be done in earth as it is in heaven. The putting on of the immortal is the first sense of resurrection; the coming again into the world in that knowledge is the second sense of resurrection, the resurrection of the body. This is the arc described by the interior movement of the contemplative's realization.

Let me be clear that in speaking of the resurrection this way, I am following my general intention of giving the *interior* interpretation of these Easter mysteries, that is, tracing the sequence of events that the revelation presents in the historical mode as being for us, in the development of our spiritual life, a sequence of "prayer" events: seeking, letting go, finding, seeing, withdrawing from the world, and returning into the world. Our resurrection experience follows — and is made possible by — our Sabbath and baptismal experience. I am saying that this is what is meant by "the resurrection of the body" in the interior or spiritual or prayer-life sense. I am not addressing the question of what happens to individuals after the death of their biological bodies.

One of the interesting things to notice in interpreting the resurrection in terms of our interior life is that resurrection is not the end of the story — just as it is not the end of the story in, for instance, the Glorious Mysteries of the Rosary, or, for that matter, in the liturgical year of the church. The bulk of the church year is devoted to working out the implications and applications of resurrection life. Our spiritual development is only partly covered by the works and graces leading up to Sabbath realization and baptismal conversion. The rest comes after that (but will not be studied in any detail in this book, which covers only the mysteries of Lent, Holy Week, and Resurrection). This is why, I often say, the resurrection occurs, not on the Sabbath, but on the first day, the first day of a new working week. It is true that what I have called the first sense of resurrection is the Sabbath, the rising up again to heavenly reality, but the second sense, vividly imaged in the New Testament and mentioned in the Apostles' Creed, "the resurrection of the body," is re-entrance into the work of the world (John 5:17). The difference is that we now look at the world and our work in it from a completely new perspective.

There is a rather curious line in one of John's resurrection stories that leads us to a prophetic vision indicating that the resurrection is a process that is just beginning. John 21:11, in the midst of an account of how the risen Jesus appears on the shore and is seen by his disciples in the fishing boat, says that on Jesus' advice they were able to catch a large number of big fish: 153 to be exact. But why be exact? This always puzzled me. If you thought you were in the presence of someone who had come back from the dead, would you sit down on the beach and count fish? That seems incredible, so the appearance of this line in the evangelist's account must be intended for another purpose.

What I think may be its meaning comes from a discovery by J. A. Emerton.[2] He put the account together with Ezekiel 47:6–12, which tells of a vision that also includes "very many different kinds of fish." In the vision Ezekiel sees "water issuing from below the threshold of the temple toward the east" — the east being the gate by which the Lord had entered the temple (44:2) — which water gradually becomes a stream and then a river deep enough to swim in. The river is bordered by trees and flows toward the Dead Sea. And "when [the river] enters the stagnant water of this Sea, the [salt] waters will become fresh" (47:8); "wherever the river goes, every living creature that swarms will live, and there will be very many fish, for this water goes there [in order] that the waters of that Sea may become fresh; so everything will live where the river goes." This is obviously a resurrection theme, but now comes the curious part.

> Fishermen will stand beside the [formerly Dead] Sea; from En-gedi [on the west side about halfway to the southern tip of the Sea] to En-eglaim [a little over a mile south of Qumran, at the northwest corner of the Sea], it will be a place for the spreading of nets; its fish will be of very many kinds, like the fish of the Great Sea [Mediterranean].
> (Ezek. 47:10)

The word we pay attention to is "Eglaim," the point where the miraculous river enters the sea and begins its revivifying work. Both Hebrew and Greek, like many languages, used the same characters for numbers as for letters — as we still use "Roman numerals" — so that an expression in letters could also be read as a number. And this letter/number exchange could be used as a code and manipulated in various ways. A common way — still extant among us as a popular "numerology" device — is adding up the number values of the letters. In Hebrew the numbers for Eglaim are E=70, G=3, La=30, I=10, M=40. The total is 153! I like to think that the mention of Eglaim's "number name" in this resurrection story emphasizes that now the transformation is beginning.

The same Ezekiel vision says that on the banks of the river there "grow all kinds of trees for food. Their leaves will not wither nor their fruit fail, but they will bear fresh fruit every month, because the water for them flows from the sanctuary. Their fruit will be for food and their leaves for healing" (47:12). The Book of Revelation repeats this vision of "the river of the water of life...flowing from the throne of God and...on either side of the river, the tree of life with its twelve kinds of fruit, yielding its fruit each month; and the leaves of the tree...for the healing of the nations" (22:1, 2). It appears yet again in one of the Odes of Solomon (composed about the same time as the Fourth Gospel), describing what is gained by Baptism:

> He took me to his Paradise, wherein...
> I contemplated blooming and fruit-bearing trees....
> Their fruits were shining....
> Their roots [were] from an immortal land.
> And a river of gladness was irrigating them,
> and the region round about them in the land of eternal life.[3]

The Second Coming

Now that we know that our "roots" are "immortal" and that we are sustained by the never-failing waters of Baptism, which turn the dead alive and life-giving, we are reconciled to taking up again the work of the world. We come again into everyday life. But the transformation is still going on, both in ourselves and in the world that we touch. It has begun in earnest and is proceeding. What is different is that we are no longer concerned to gain eternal life for ourselves. We have that, we know it, we are sure of it. And because of that confidence, "faith," we turn our attention and concern to manifesting the divine life in the forms of cosmic reality. We are looking now from a point of view that is rooted in our sense of our own reality in God. It makes everything look quite new to us, and our new ability to offer love-and-meaning energy to our world helps it to become "new" (Rom. 6:4; Rev. 21:5).

Now what was concentrated in the unity and invisibility of the Formless comes consciously through us into the forms of manifestation.

" . . . for nothing is covered that will not be revealed, or
hidden that will not be known. What I tell you in the dark,
utter in the light; and what you hear whispered, proclaim
upon the housetops." (Matt. 10:27)

We are reminded that "to you it has been given to know the
secrets of the kingdom of God" (Luke 8:10), and that therefore we should "take heed . . . how you hear; for to one who has
more will be given, and from one who has not, even what he
thinks he has will be taken away" (Luke 8:18). The mystical
union with the Absolute in the darkness of the Great Sabbath
has resulted in enlightenment, and what was realized wordlessly
then, we now must translate into shared speech.

If we do this well, we will see still more deeply; if we neglect
the vision and do not incarnate it, we may well lose it. When
Jesus raised the daughter of Jairus to new life, "he directed that
something should be given her to eat" (Luke 8:55). We have to
keep feeding our resurrection experience.

One of the most important worlds that we come back into
again is the world of language and other symbolic expressions.
It is noteworthy that one of the very first things the risen Jesus
did was to explain the Scriptures. This occurs in the resurrection story of the disciples on the road to Emmaus (Luke 24:27,
also 45). After direct personal experience, the symbolic indica-
tions of the tradition are much more meaningful; indeed, they
may make sense for the first time. Where words had been used
to point us toward experience, the words helping us to the experience, now the experience is primary and the words secondary:
we have the experience and we express it symbolically and
recognize when others have symbolized it. All sorts of things
suddenly become expressive in their various forms of the central reality we entered in the wordless realm. When the disciples
and their Scripture teacher reached Emmaus, they had supper
together; the stranger took the bread, blessed and broke it —
the simplest, everyday gesture/event — and suddenly the disciples *knew.* They saw the whole thing; they saw through the

transparency, recognized the Word, recognized it so thoroughly that its symbolic mode disappeared, while the joy of its reality remained (Luke 24:31–32).

Before our enlightenment, our words are tortured as we try to stretch them this way and that to say the Unsayable. Finally the Word dies of this torture, and for us the veil of the Sanctuary is rent. And then the Word comes back again, but in a different way. It is not readily recognizable. It shows itself here and there suddenly. It doesn't follow the rules, but appears differently to different people, ignoring the usual barriers. It is unrestrained by time and space, uncontrolled by causation and objectification. Words are no longer re-presenting external objects and events, but are expressing internal reality and thereby, in a sense, creating their own world. The appearances are flowing creatively from the reality.

This power touches everything. Enlightenment manifests itself in every situation. It is as though everything received a new name (Rev. 2:17; 3:12) and is singing a new song (Rev. 5:9; 14:3). We ourselves are drinking the new wine together in the kingdom (Matt. 26:29; Mark 14:25) and speaking in new languages (Mark 16:17). We see a new world (2 Pet. 3:13) run by a new law (John 13:34). Everything that we perceive "in Christ" is a "new creation; the old has passed away [and] the new has come" (2 Cor. 5:17). The world now is seen by us in a "new and living way" as the "flesh" of God (Heb. 10:20).

In this second coming of the creative Word (including now ourselves, united to it) into the world of forms and relations and conditions, we see everything inverted and reversed. The reality in which we are embedded is not so much a matter of our trying to leave the world and get to God as of God "trying" to become the world and bring the world to a realization of being the Incarnation of God. The Incarnation, instead of being a means to the rescue of lost, sinful humanity, is an end in itself, to which all of the world's developmental ups and downs are the unavoidable, unpredictable, but still creative means.

Divine reality, God, is clearly heavily invested in the world.

> For thus God loved the cosmos, so much that he gave the
> Son, the Only One [*monogenēs*], so that the whole world,
> believing in him, would not be allowed to perish, but
> would have eternal life. (John 3:16, somewhat creatively
> interpreted)

The world is here because God wants it to be here. God is
trying to make something out of it. And we, now that we
have realized our roots in the immortal, our status as children
of God, are deeply involved in this project, not just as that
which is being formed, but also on the side of the One doing
the forming. St. Paul says that "All things are of God, of the
One having reconciled us to himself through Christ and having
given us the ministry of reconciliation" (2 Cor. 5:18). "Reconciliation" means a change from enmity to friendship, but in
the background is the meaning of "giving in exchange," even
of a "profit" coming from this exchange. We are involved in
this profitable exchange and unification, in which the world
comes to itself, to awakened consciousness of being God's self-
expression, and thus "comes back" to God. And by the same
movement God is more fully in the world as the world, that is,
incarnate.

It is this mutual indwelling or nondualism of the aspect of
forming and the aspect of being formed that seems to me to be
much of the point of the whole creative effort. I like to think
of the Creation as the "Theotokos Project,"[4] the "God-Bearer
Project." Can the divine "We" of Genesis 1:26 in fact "make
[the cosmos] in our image, after our likeness," in the image and
likeness of the Infinite? Can a relative and conditioned being
bear the values of the Absolute Unconditioned? Can the child
of God in turn give birth to God? That is what I think of as
the "profitable exchange," the "reconciliation" of the world
to God.

The Project — which I see as genuinely experimental, deeply
artistic, and thoroughly loving — involves making something
such that it can/does make itself, that is, "have life in itself" and

be able to communicate that power. The divine presence, as the creative Logos, is incarnate in the cosmos from the beginning, always entirely immanent, not an external force or external guide or plan or pattern or intervention. Thus the creation is a self-organizing, internally connected and communicating, adjusting and adaptive, emergent cosmos that we can also call, from a religious point of view, "the beloved child in whom the Parent delights" (Matt. 3:17).

The *monogenēs theos* of John 1:18 "exegetes" the internal reality of the invisible God. It develops the world by being the world, which grows from within. It is not an outside force governing the world but is the very internal, intrinsic dynamic of the world itself, that which is developing, the union of the doer and the done. That is what it means to be self-organizing, having life in oneself. Having become the world, the *monogenēs theos* truly, genuinely is the world, in the world's own proper, natural, limited, nearly chaotic, sometimes catastrophic, unpredictable way. The early church was insistent on upholding the full, real, ordinary, common humanity of Christ as well as the fullness of his divinity. If this Christology is extended beyond the single individual man "hypodigm" (John 13:15), we have a grand view of the significance of the world.

The world is not just a creature — merely a "man" created and blessed by God. Neither is the world a pure illusion masking the Absolute God, an appearance without any nature of its own or an unaccountable dream that vanishes when one awakes. And God is not just an invisible and formless spirit in a transcendent realm totally other than the world. The full reality is the Invisible generating the *monogenēs theos,* which, as Incarnate Exegete, grows up as the cosmos, experimentally, artistically, lovingly, advancing in age and consciousness (Luke 2:52) together with difficulties and setbacks (Mark 10:30), exploring to "see if" it can become more and more the "image and likeness" of the divine Parent. But not of the divine Parent alone, for it comes as it grows to "favor" both its parents, "God" and "man" or nature (Luke 2:52).

This is the full Incarnation. When we, who are internal and integral to this enterprise — elements in the huge Body — see that this is what is going on, when we feel the divine presence, will, commitment, love, when we know how important and precious the world is to God and know what we ourselves are because of our position in this reality, then we know that we have "eternal life." This is what "believing in" Christ means (John 3:16).

The Kingdom on Earth

This "believing" is made manifest in "works," because we are members of the Incarnate Exegete — exegeting is our business. The Epistle of James reminds us that our self-realization is to be expressed by creative acts in the world, as befits those who are incorporated into the creative Word and are therefore "doers of the Word." We have "looked into the perfect law, the law of liberty," and we "will be blessed in [our] doing" (James 1:22–25).

One of the most important areas in which this is true is the community or social area, and there are many eloquent voices speaking for our vocation in this area. I want to quote two of these voices, saying very well what truly follows from everything that we have developed so far. The first is Jon Sobrino, liberation theologian, speaking from the context of the struggle of the poor and powerless in Latin America:

> If persons and communities follow Jesus and proclaim the kingdom of God to the poor; if they strive for liberation from every kind of slavery; if they seek, for all human beings, especially for that immense majority of men and women who are crucified persons, a life in conformity with the dignity of daughters and sons of God; if they have the courage and forthrightness to speak the truth... if, in the discipleship of Jesus, they effectuate their own conver-

sion from being oppressor to being men and women of service ... if in doing justice they seek peace and in making peace they seek to base it on justice; and if they do all this in the following and discipleship of Jesus because he did all this himself — then they believe in Jesus.[5]

Robert A. Ludwig, who also cites this passage, follows it with warm words of his own:

One moves from the reign of fear to the reign of God, from being controlled by the powers that be to a freedom from such control. In and through Jesus' liberation, one steps over boundaries, taking a place where one "doesn't belong," according to convention. Taking responsibility for one's own body and sitting at the table with whoever is hungry, refusing to honor the proper hierarchies and discriminations, overcoming the polarities that segment and separate — this is the faith of Jesus. It is healing, precisely because one's allegiance and trust is *singular* [*iḥidaya*] ... only God reigns! To believe is to be set free from pretensions.[6]

I myself have talked about what I call the "Holy Thursday Revolution," the core of which I set forth in the chapter on the Body of Christ. This is a vision of what we can be, what we may say we feel "called" to be. It seems to be a very long-term project. It is my opinion that in order to be free to do the truly revolutionary thing, we have first to enter into the mystical emptiness of the Sabbath. And on the other hand, once we have been renewed by that discovery of our divine filiation, then we must incarnate that truth. If the Exegete, the Creative Word, is present in the world as Becoming, as process, then we must "believe in" Holy Becoming, in process, in growth, and in our own participation in that whole growth process, both as those who are growing and as those who somehow share the power to enable and direct growth.

Another very important area in which we incarnate the vision we gain in the baptismal transformation is the area we call environmental concern, or ecological virtue. It is our care for the whole planet as a very important part of God's "Theotokos Project." We do not yet know whether we human beings are the only highly conscious beings in the universe, or whether Earth is one among many living and conscious planets. We must do the very best we can to protect and enhance life and the conditions for life on this planet, which is alive. We cannot limit our frame of concern to our particular selves and families, our business, our stockholders, our national interest. The picture of reality is much, much vaster than that.

Our ecological philosophy/theology can be developed out of what seems to be a basic insight stemming from Jesus, another instance of how he reverses and inverts things. Instead of taking as the norm of reality those things that are *outside* one another, he takes as standard and paradigm those that are *in* one another. The Incarnation in its fullness is the incarnation of the Trinity, of the communitarian nondualism that is the ultimate reality.[7] And the mystery of Holy Communion expresses it in its essential "in one another" character (John 14:20): the mutually feeding, mutually indwelling community, in which all members give themselves to one another as food, for the sake of life, abundant life.

The whole universe is structured and organized in such a way that all members depend on one another; they are all, in fact, dynamic processes constituted precisely by their relations to one another. It is exactly the Trinity that the universe images, which it incarnates, embodies, phenomenalizes, shows forth, reveals, exegetes, glorifies. The universe puts into flesh, into matter, the Trinitarian perichoretic life, the differentiation by relation, the self-sharing, the dynamic unity by which the nature of God is expressed. All the beings and events of the cosmos are interacting, interdependent, life-sharing, living-together. It is a symbiotic cosmos.[8]

Ecology has as its hallmark the principle that no one species is the species from whose viewpoint the whole is to be understood and appreciated. Since no member of the system is to be seen as the system's master, the motto of such a deepened sense of ecology could well be "all of you are brethren" (Matt. 23:8). The basic moral virtue would be respect — the minimal degree of self-giving love — accorded every member.

The deeper sense of biological ecology holds that our obligation to protect the environment is not based on our need or desire to preserve things in good working order only for ourselves and our descendents — so that our grandchildren will inherit unpolluted air, water, and land and will still be able to enjoy seeing a variety of animals and plants. No, our obligation to protect the environment is based on the *rights* of the creatures who compose the ecosystem to their own lives and on the value of cooperating with the natural movement of the planet in terms of the good of the whole.

Indeed, we shouldn't even speak of "the environment," because that implies a privileged viewpoint, the viewpoint of the species whose "environment" it is deemed to be, whereas we propose a commitment to an ecological morality that abjures such privilege. Instead of saying that we human beings are the only really valuable or meaningful beings on the planet and that everything else exists as our "support system," put here by a thoughtful Deity for our convenience and pleasure, we seek a view in which *all* creatures compose the whole system together, in which all are valuable and significant. In such a view the living ecosystem is dependent on, and must be respectful of, all of them. "You are brethren, all of you."

St. Francis of Assisi seems to have had this vision, expressed in his "Canticle to the Sun." Perhaps he was proposing an alternative Christian view of nature and of the position of humanity within it. He was moving, I would say (in the terms of the Holy Thursday Revolution), to replace the "domination paradigm" of footwashing with the "communion paradigm" of life-sharing, seeing a larger interpretation of the metaphor of the Christ-Vine than his tradition had usually offered. He saw the Eucharistic Planet. He was able to see it because he had first embraced humility and spiritual poverty — emptiness, the apophatic way to the realization of the Absolute. Coming out from that point of view again into creation, into the resurrection of the body, he was able to see the real presence of the Divine in everything and to know that "whatever you do to the least of these my brethren, you do to me" (Matt. 25:40).[9]

Coming back to our small private selves in very ordinary daily life, we also incarnate the Wondrous Being. One of the most striking things that happens to us in our resurrection of the body is that tiny, trivial things seem beautiful and marvelous — which, indeed, they are, as we recognize when we take time to study them carefully. Such a humble and common thing as water is almost miraculous in its varied properties, so essential to our survival. We should all read up just a little chemistry and biology, enough to appreciate what we and the rest of the world are, what artistry and orderly connections we find all about us, how astonishing the complex world is.

When we take a little time to remember to look, to marvel, we find that there are sources of joy, of esthetic delight, of quiet happiness on every hand. We discover that it is literally true that when our eye is single (*ihidaya*) our whole body is full of light. Bruno Barnhart, in his *The Good Wine,* has a fantasy of what the catechist might say to the newly baptized, if we instructed and initiated our converts in the fullness of the mysteries:

> The God who said, "Let light shine out of darkness," has shone in your heart, and you have seen that the light is good.... You have heard within your heart (the voice of your Parent), saying to you, "You are my beloved child; in you I am well pleased." ... Now you hear the story of the life of Jesus in a new way, because the light that was in him is in you.... From this light which is within you, the creation of the world begins again.[10]

To be in the kingdom, says Jesus, is to be a child again (Mark 10:13–16). While this saying has several true interpretations, one we might think of here is how — if we had a reasonably happy childhood — we were able to enjoy very simple things in a kind of eternity. Thich Nhat Hanh, the Vietnamese Buddhist monk and poet, tells of how, at age four, he would take most of an hour to nibble a cookie, seated on the earth, looking up at the sky, sheltered by the bamboo thicket, kept company by the flowers, his cat, and his dog. Most of us have memories like that. Real Baptism opens us to that experience again. The "cookie of our childhood" is still there, hidden in our heart, as are a million other tiny sources of pure happiness, and if we are attentive, we will see and enjoy them.[11]

And our joy is not confined to ourselves but radiates out to all. Just as Jesus intended to enter into us, that his joy might be in us and our joy might be full (John 15:11), so neither can we contain our joy: our peace and happiness envelop all those around us. When we interact with people — or circumstances — we do not feel drained of energy, as we did when we were still obliged to protect and defend our ego-self. Perceiving creative action and interaction as reality itself, we feel ourselves fully living, full of the richness of God's life, the interior fountain that never fails.[12]

The divine life now becomes natural for us, no longer something to be compared to an alternative. We are really "saved" when we no longer think of ourselves as "saved," because there is no alternative. This is when profound incarnation takes place. The reality of God is intensely perceived as present in everything. The world is truly charged, as Gerard Manley Hopkins said, "with the grandeur of God." The kingdom is hidden right here, even in the passions and illusions of our superficial consciousness. When we are shaken awake, we see it. All things are "epiphanies of the rapture of being."[13]

Exercises

This is a general meditation and practice that you can continue to use throughout the rest of the liturgical year.

1. If you have had some significant breakthroughs in the course of doing these Lenten/Easter practices, give some practical thought now to how you are going to "nourish" your resurrection experience, keep it alive, enable it to grow. What will you read, think about, meditate on; what spiritual practices will you do? What distractions arising in the culture and in your former habits will you now avoid?

2. Renew your stability in the wordless state, in the Sabbath Paradise of "this day." Then be aware of your resurrection in the body, aware of the largeness of the world, the complexity of chemical and biological forms, the intricate net of mutual dependence in which all created beings affect one another. Allow yourself to marvel at this and to rejoice in its wonder and beauty. (It is also all right to resolve to learn more about it!) See the sacramental, the *mystery,* aspect of everything around you or that you know of.

3. In the larger social, political, ecological contexts, is there anything you can do? Think about it, maybe read about it, inquire about it, talk to other people about it. Try to see how all of us, sharing in one another's lives as a community, are actually participating in the planet-process. How can we do it better, to help the Theotokos develop? Remember to allow for apparently adverse circumstances to be material for creative transformation.

4. Feel your union with the God whose first name is I AM and whose second name is MAY YOU BE. Situate yourself in this place where Absolute Transcendent Being and creative generosity are a single Reality. This is true of *you;* this is the secret of your own being. Feel *centered* here. Being centered in this way, then open yourself to the divine creativity, to the will that many should be, be various, be expanding, growing, fruitful, transforming, unifying. Take the position of one who is enthusiastically helping to create this world. Live in this prayer attitude of appreciation, centeredness, and creative outpouring. Feel the richness of our God-with-us life.

EPILOGUE

THE GOSPEL OF JOHN warns us, "I have yet many things to say to you, but you cannot bear them now" (John 16:12). We may believe that this will go on indefinitely. How can the finite world ever enunciate all that the Infinite has to say? So there will always be further truth and wonder and beauty to discover. More mysteries to render up their secrets. More insights to gain. We tell one another what we have seen in gazing into the mysteries. We see different things. Why not? The mysteries are deep and rich. They are manna for our souls. The manna can be prepared in various ways (Num. 11:8) but is always nourishing. It sustains us during the journey through the wilderness.

> When the people of Israel saw it, they said to one another, "What is it?" For they did not know what it was. And Moses said to them, "It is the bread which the Lord has given you to eat.... Gather of it, each of you, as much as you can eat."... And the people... gathered, some more, some less. But... one who gathered much had nothing over, and one who gathered little had no lack; each gathered according to what each could eat. (Exod. 16:15–18)

This is how it is with the mysteries. Even when we do not fully comprehend what they have to teach, we are fed by them. Each of us takes as much as we can digest and assimilate, and this suits each of us; we are fed at that time according to our power to receive. As our appetite and power to receive increase, so does the divine bread; there is no shortage (see Matt. 16:9).

> He commanded the skies above, and opened the doors of heaven; and he rained down upon them manna to eat, and gave them the grain of heaven. Human beings ate the bread of the angels; he sent them food in abundance. (Ps. 78:23–25)

NOTES

Chapter 1: The Sacred Mysteries

1. Ronald Knox, *The Window in the Wall: Reflections on the Holy Eucharist* (New York: Sheed & Ward, 1957); Edwin Bernbaum, *The Way to Shambhala: A Search for the Mythical Kingdom beyond the Himalayas* (Los Angeles: Tarcher, 1980), 135.

2. 1QS 4:20–22; Frank Moore Cross, Jr., *The Ancient Library of Qumran and Modern Biblical Studies* (Garden City, N.Y.: Anchor, 1961), 100. There is a section here on "Common Theological Language: The Gospel of John" that may be of further interest. "1QS" stands for "The Section Rule of the Community."

3. A. J. Wensinck, *Mystic Treatises of Isaac of Nineveh,* trans. from Bedjan's Syriac text with an Introduction and Registers (Wiesbaden: Saendig, 1969), 8.

Chapter 2: Prayer and Fasting

1. I take this apt expression from Masao Abe, perhaps assisted by his editor Steven Heine, in *A Study of Dōgen: His Philosophy and Religion* (Albany: State University of New York Press, 1992), 111.

Chapter 3: Our Secret Self

1. W. Norris Clarke, S.J., *The Philosophical Approach to God: A Neo-Thomist Perspective* (Winston-Salem, N.C.: Wake Forest University Press, 1979), 26 (see also the preceding pages on the dynamism of the will).

2. A useful image is of the molecules of iron in a magnet: instead of being in confusion, turned in every possible direction, they are all lined up, facing the same way, their collective "pull" making the bar of iron

now a magnet that can move other things, can do work. Similarly, our emotional, affective, volitional energies, which are often helter-skelter and pulling against one another and fatiguing us by their confusion and contradiction, can fall into a meaningful pattern, organizing themselves so that satisfying and successful action results. This "calming" or "taming" does not have the effect of weakening but on the contrary of strengthening, as an athlete or musician or dancer learns to control the body to accomplish extraordinary feats of skill and beauty.

Chapter 6: The Spiritual Journey as the Way of the Cross

1. Max Oliva, S.J., *Free to Pray/Free to Love* (Notre Dame, Ind.: Ave Maria Press, 1994), 31ff.

Chapter 7: The Death of the Word

1. Thomas Merton, *New Seeds of Contemplation* (New York: New Directions, 1961), 35.
2. C. F. Kelley, *Meister Eckhart on Divine Knowledge* (New Haven: Yale University Press, 1977), 26, quoting Eckhart, *Die deutschen Werke* 1:35–40.
3. Ludwig von Bertalanffy, *A Systems View of Man,* ed. Paul A. LaViolette (Boulder, Colo.: Westview, 1981), 76.
4. Franklin Merrell-Wolff, *The Philosophy of Consciousness without an Object* (New York: Julian, 1983), 79–80; Masao Abe, *A Study of Dōgen: His Philosophy and Religion,* ed. Steven Heine (Albany: State University of New York Press, 1992), 157.
5. Kelley, *Meister Eckhart,* 30.

Chapter 8: The Great Sabbath

1. Gershom Scholem, *Kabbalah* (New York: New American Library, 1974), 46.
2. Ibid., 94ff.
3. Carol Carruth Johnson, review of *Leisure, A Spiritual Need,* by Leonard Doohan (Notre Dame, Ind.: Ave Maria Press, 1990), quoting Doohan, in *Weavings* 8, no. 2 (March/April 1993): 43.
4. These ideas are developed in Josef Pieper, *Leisure: The Basis of Culture,* trans. Alexander Dru (New York: Pantheon, 1952).
5. Erich Fromm, *You Shall Be as Gods* (Greenwich, Conn.: Fawcett, 1969), 156.

6. *The Union Prayerbook for Jewish Worship,* Part I (New York: Central Conference of American Rabbis, 1961), 27.

7. See Scholem, *Kabbalah,* 19ff.

8. Bruno Barnhart, *The Good Wine: Reading John from the Center* (New York: Paulist Press, 1993), 111.

Chapter 9: Baptismal Transformation

1. Ignatius of Antioch, *Epistle to the Trallians,* chap. 5, and *Epistle to the Ephesians,* chap. 3, Clarke's Ante-Nicene Library, vol. 1. Ignatius, who was a fellow-disciple of Polycarp, died about 110 C.E.

2. Clement of Alexandria, *Stromata* (available in collections of the Ante-Nicene Fathers), bk. 1, chap. 1, and bk. 6, chap. 15.

3. Origen, *Against Celsus,* bk. 4, chap. 16.

4. Ibid., bk. 5, chap. 29.

5. Origen, *De Principiis,* Preface.

6. Origen, *Against Celsus,* bk. 3, chap. 9.

7. See, e.g., Edwin Bernbaum, *The Way to Shambhala* (Los Angeles: Tarcher, 1980), 208, 212.

8. I am indebted to Hilda Montalvo for developing this thought: "From Outside In to Inside Out," manuscript in progress. See also Eugene H. Peterson, "Rhythms of Grace," *Weavings* 8, no. 2 (March/April 1993): 17–18.

9. See B. Bruteau, "The Immaculate Conception, Our Original Face," *Cross Currents* 39, no. 2 (Summer 1989); reprinted in Bruteau, *What We Can Learn from the East* (New York: Crossroad, 1995).

10. Aphrahat, *Demonstrations,* quoted in Gabriele Winkler, "The Origins and Idiosyncrasies of the Earliest Form of Asceticism," in *The Continuing Quest for God,* ed. William Skudlarek (Collegeville, Minn.: Liturgical Press, 1981), 13.

11. Robert Murray, *Symbols of Church and Kingdom: A Study in Early Syriac Tradition,* 2d ed. (Cambridge: University Press, 1975), 13.

12. Winkler, "The Origins and Idiosyncrasies of the Earliest Form of Asceticism," 33.

13. Hymns on the Epiphany, No. 8, quoted in Murray, *Symbols of Church and Kingdom,* 16.

14. See, e.g., James 1:8, 4:8; Luke 12:28–29; Matthew 14:31, 21:21; Mark 11:23. See B. Bruteau, "Following Jesus into Faith," *The Journal of Christian Healing* 10, no. 2 (Fall 1988).

15. Matthew 9:22; Mark 5:34, 10:52; Luke 8:48, 17:19; and others.

16. Winkler, "The Origins and Idiosyncrasies of the Earliest Form of Asceticism."

17. Bruno Barnhart, *The Good Wine: Reading John from the Center* (New York: Paulist Press, 1993), 416, no. 119.

Chapter 10: The Resurrection of the Body

1. See Gospel of Thomas, Logion 49: "You shall find the kingdom; because you come from it, and you shall go there again."

2. J. A. Emerton, "The Hundred and Fifty-Three Fishes in John XXI.11," *Journal of Theological Studies* 9 (1958): 86–89.

3. *The Odes of Solomon,* trans. and ed. J. H. Charlesworth, Society of Biblical Literature Texts and Translations 13, Pseudepigrapha Series 7 (Missoula, Mont.: Scholars Press, 1978), Ode 11.

4. B. Bruteau, "The Theotokos Project," in *Embracing Earth: Catholic Approaches to Ecology,* ed. Albert J. LaChance and John E. Carroll (Maryknoll, N.Y.: Orbis Books, 1994).

5. Jon Sobrino, *Jesus in Latin America* (Maryknoll, N.Y.: Orbis Books, 1982), 53–54.

6. Robert A. Ludwig, "Reconstructing Jesus for a Dysfunctional Church," in *Jesus and Faith: A Conversation on the Work of John Dominic Crossan,* ed. Jeffrey Carlson and Robert A. Ludwig (Maryknoll, N.Y.: Orbis Books, 1994), 67.

7. B. Bruteau, "Communitarian Nondualism," in *The Other Half of My Soul: Bede Griffiths and the Hindu-Christian Dialogue,* ed. Beatrice Bruteau (Wheaton, Ill.: Quest Books, 1996).

8. B. Bruteau, *Symbiotic Cosmos,* serialized from 1991 to 1994 in *The Roll,* publication of the Schola Contemplationis, 3425 Forest Lane, Pfafftown, NC 27040.

9. The paragraphs on ecology are reprinted from my "Eucharistic Ecology and Ecological Spirituality," *Cross Currents* 40, no. 4 (Winter 1990): 505–8.

10. Bruno Barnhart, *The Good Wine: Reading John from the Center* (New York: Paulist Press, 1993), 347.

11. Thich Nhat Hanh, *Peace Is Every Step: The Path of Mindfulness in Everyday Life,* ed. Arnold Kotler (New York: Bantam, 1992), 20–21.

12. Chogyam Trungpa, *Cutting through Spiritual Materialism,* ed. John Baker and Marvin Casper (Boulder, Colo.: Shambhala, 1973), 99.

13. Joseph Campbell, *The Inner Reaches of Outer Space* (New York: Harper & Row, 1986), 19.